SEEN AND HEARD

CONTENTS

FOREWORD

Jackie Cray has written a strong plea to the churches to see children as people in their own right, and most certainly not as nuisances. She points out that the children in the congregation have as many gifts and abilities as the adults and, in this lively book, we are told how both children and adults can participate and contribute in worship.

I am increasingly convinced that the churches have to put children at the top of their priorities and this requires concern, not only about children's activities, but also about the creation of church services where children can feel welcome and can participate. Jackie Cray's book *Seen and Heard*, based on long experience at St Michael le Belfry, York, will not only give good ideas but also stimulate the right sort of thinking.

† Gavin Maidstone

CHAPTER ONE

WHAT IF . . . ?

I often ask myself, what would it be like if children were welcome in our churches to be both *seen* and *heard*? What if children were invited to take part in the *whole* life of the church and not just in the occasional church service? What if children were valued and recognised in the liturgical, pastoral and financial structures of the church, in terms of planning, resources and decision-making? What if children were allowed to *contribute* to the whole life of the church? What difference would this make to the shape and form of the church as we know it today?

On the road

In recent years I have spent a lot of time travelling as part of my work for the Families and Under Fives ministry of The Church Pastoral Aid Society. It has been my privilege to visit many different churches, meeting many different men, women and children – vicars, worship leaders, parents, retired people, teenagers, toddlers and babies.

Afterwards, as I drive home, the long hours behind the wheel give me plenty of opportunity to think about where I've been and what I've seen – so many different situations, but in all of them I find God's people deeply committed to the work of service and caring, mission and outreach. All in their different ways are seeking to be Christ's church in this turbulent, end-of-century world.

I meet many people who work with children and young people, and I take a particular interest in how these children and their older brothers and sisters are welcomed, taught and encouraged in their churches. Sometimes I'm astonished by the wonderful things I discover – young people taking part in the full life of their church, receiving from *and* giving to their fellow Christians. At other times I'm dispirited, asking myself why some churches have never addressed the most basic questions about how they value and receive their children. Why are the children there in the first place? What is their significance? How should they be treated?

Often as I drive, I ponder on these many situations and questions, sometimes agonising over a particularly tough problem, or allowing myself to feel the pain and struggle of some of my fellow Christians working in difficult and challenging circumstances. At other times I'm equally inspired by the creativity, 'wild hope' and sheer 'getting on with the job' determination of many of the people I meet.

As well as reflecting on individual situations and encounters, sometimes I ponder on the larger questions of how, as a body of believers, we are to *be* the church – adults and children, young and old together in today's changing world. And sometimes I let my imagination roll ...

What if there really were churches which welcomed children to share in the whole life of the church, gave them value and significance and encouraged them to contribute to and participate in services? What would Sunday morning at such a church be like?

A perfectly ordinary church

St William's Parish Church is a perfectly ordinary church in a perfectly ordinary suburb. This church of my imagination brings together good ideas I have seen around the country and innovative people I have met. Unfortunately, they are not to be found under one roof as yet, but this is the report I would like to have written.

I visited St William's recently to find out about 'All Together', the series of 'all-age' Sunday morning services which they launched a little over a year ago. I enjoyed my visit immensely. Everyone was friendly and welcoming. I was neither ignored nor made to feel conspicuous – just the right balance.

What did I think of the service? It's enough to say that I was impressed. Afterwards I took time to talk to a cross-section of the congregation. I wanted to know how they felt about 'All Together', about the difference it made to them and about how they felt its introduction had affected the church as a whole.

'Next week I'm bringing my guinea pig'

Ben Simpson is a nine-year-old, high-energy phenomenon. He is not exactly hyperactive, just bursting with interest, enthusiasm and that kind of sparky self-confidence that seems to disappear with the arrival of adolescence. Once I'd got his attention, I found that he had plenty to say about 'All Together'.

'Most of it I like,' said Ben. 'Some bits are brilliant. A few bits are boring – luckily they don't last very long. It's good that the bits I do like don't just happen and then disappear. They happen every week and you can look forward to them.

'My favourites are "Hot Spot" and "Zingy Thingy". After we've sung the first song, Alf – he's one of the leaders – gets us all to sing the "Hot Spot" song: "Hot Spot! Hot Spot! Should you do it, or should you not?" Dad says it's not really a proper song, just a catchy jingle – but he still sings it in the car on the way home. Then, while we're all singing, Alf zooms off the stage and drags someone out of their seat. They always pretend like crazy that they don't want to come, but he always manages to get them up to the front. Last week it was Mrs French, my teacher. She had to stand in the middle and then we all shouted: "Do it or not? Do it or not? No escape from the spot that's *hot*!" We always shout that last "*hot*" very, very loud! At the same time, a big orange spot comes down from high up in the roof and stops just behind the victim's head. Then Alf asks the Hot Spot "Question of the Week". For Mrs French it was all about being in the check-out line at the supermarket and being given too much change (a whole £5 too much) by accident.

'What should she do? Smile quietly and keep the cash? Come back tomorrow and sort it out when the place isn't so busy? Or should she give the money back, even though there's a long line of people waiting and the new girl on the till will feel very embarrassed when Mrs French points out her mistake? Alf explains the problem again and we all have to be really quiet while his giant stop-watch counts off the "Thirty Second Think". Then Mrs French has to write down what she has decided and she hands the piece of paper over to Alf.

'Next comes the bit I really like. Alf jumps off the platform and brings the rover mike down to find out what *we* think. This week I put my hand up because I wanted to tell Alf about what Dad did at McDonald's when we got three extra portions of fries that we hadn't ordered – or paid for.

'Alf lets everyone have a say, even the grannies – but you have to be quick. This bit is called the "Two Minute Scoot". Then he goes back to the platform, we all do the "Hot Spot" shout again and he reads out what the victim wrote down a few minutes before. Sometimes it's easy to guess what they will decide – but not always. After that we always have a short prayer, asking Jesus to help us next time we need to choose to do the right thing, even though doing it might make us look stupid in front of our friends.

'Next week's Hot Spot question is "Do animals go to heaven?" and the person on the spot will be the vicar. I'm going to ask if I can bring Pipsqueak, my guinea pig, to church with me.

'Later on we always have the "Zingy Thingy" bit of the morning. Lizzie (she and Alf are in charge of "All Together") has a big yellow bag in which the "thing with zing" is hidden. This week it turned out to be a packet of rice. Lizzie always tries to get people to guess what makes it special, because the point of the thing in the bag is that it has "zing" – something about it which makes it important to somebody in the church – and important to God as well. When there have been three of four guesses, Lizzie invites its owner to come up to the front.

'It turned out that the rice belonged to Richard Johnson. He has been working with Tear Fund on a farm project in Bangladesh. He explained how the people depend completely on there being a good rice harvest every year. Richard is a plant expert and he is helping the farmers use the best kind of rice plants for their soil and weather. He showed us pictures of the farming family he stayed with – Anil and Gupta, their four children and their two grannies who live with them. Then we prayed for them. Every time we have "All Together" there's a different "Zingy Thingy". It's nearly always a surprise and it's usually interesting.

'The rest of "All Together" is OK. There's nearly always a drama sketch, which is usually funny, but sometimes it can make you think as well. It's easy to join in with the prayers because Alf and Lizzie put them up in big, clear writing on the overhead projector screen. Sometimes there are pictures to remind you of what we are praying about. Alf says you don't have to keep your eyes closed if you don't want to. Most of the pictures are drawn by Tom, who is Lizzie's brother. He's a brilliant cartoonist. Last Easter he did a whole series of shadow pictures about Jesus dying on the cross and rising again. The band played quiet music while some people read the story out loud. I remember everything went very still and quiet.

'When you go in to "All Together" someone gives you a notice sheet. You don't get any other books because there are already Bibles on the seats and all the other words go up on the screen.

13

Dad says he's glad he doesn't have to juggle any more with three or four different books. I like the news-sheet as well because there are always some puzzles on it. So, if you feel a boredom attack coming on you can always do the wordsearch.

'Last week, my Gran's home group were in charge of the middle part of "All Together" – that's the bit where there's usually a drama sketch and the main talk. Most of them were really old like Gran. She acted in the sketch. I'd never seen her do anything like that before. She was brilliant.'

Moderately cool

Kate Simpson, Ben's big sister, is fifteen. In leggings, baggy jumper and Doc Marten boots, she is conventionally unconventional. Behind the so-casual exterior, she's a bright, thoughtful young woman, quietly eager to find out how she fits in to the church.

'"All Together"? Actually, it's OK,' says Kate. 'If you'd asked me a year ago you would probably have got a very different answer. I thought it was going to be just for the little kids. I mean, I knew Ben would enjoy it because he's Mr Enthusiasm. If Alf or Lizzie asks for a volunteer, Ben's hand practically shoots through the ceiling and he gets that weird, desperate-for-attention, please-choose-me look – you know? Typical nine-year-old, I suppose.

'At first I put "All Together" down as a potential MYZ (Major Yawn Zone). I thought: here we go, the zappy, snappy, middle-class, let's-all-pretend-we're-one-big-happy-family show – a kind of spiritual *Sesame Street*. Brain death or what? If we're really unlucky it may involve the curate wearing his Hawaiian shirt and doing his "Hey, I'm cool" routine, the one that takes you to a place beyond embarrassment.

'So that's why the first bit of good news was that most of the services were going to be run by Alf and Lizzie. They aren't particularly young (I think Alf is thirty-four) but they're funny and moderately cool, without trying too hard, if you know what I mean. They don't force people to join in. For instance, they'd never dream of doing what someone here (I name no names) once did: stopping everybody in the middle of a song and saying, "Hey, *come on*, this isn't how they sang it at Spring Harvest! Let's start again. Especially you teens over there." Can you believe it? *Teens?* I mean, like *crush* us, we're worms. I think the good thing about Alf and Liz is that they are kind of normal, but fun. They link all the different parts of the service together, a bit like the presenters on one of the Saturday morning magazine programmes on television. Of course, some of the items are aimed very much at Ben's age-group, with lots of noise and joining in. Actually quite a few of them are a good laugh. But not everything is at *Blue Peter* level.

'For the last few weeks there's been a five-minute segment called "News Shot". It's a kind of video compilation of items from the TV news, usually focusing on a particular theme. So far it's been about unemployment, street people and the Aids crisis in Africa. It usually comes just before the main prayers. I think it's good because it's about real-life problems. The pictures stay in my mind and really help me to think when we start to pray.

'A while back Alf and Liz came along to our "Fifteen Plus" Wednesday group. We talked about things we liked and didn't like about "All Together". They wanted to know if we had any suggestions for improving it. They're good listeners.

'Well, out of that has come a new short segment called "Green Scene". It's about environmental issues, local and international. We got some excellent ideas from the Tear Fund "God's Earth" project. As well as making people in the church more aware of good things like recycling, "Green Scene" gives the Wednesday group a chance to take part in a way that's useful and doesn't make you cringe. And Alf and Liz *never* comment about what you're wearing. Last week one of my Gran's friends came up to me after the service: "I hadn't realised before that the Bible had so much to say about these things!" That's what she said.'

'Avoiding the "Triple C" factor'

Tom Gibbons, a thirty-six-year-old graphic designer, has been part of St Will's for six years. His quirky cartoon pictures add humour and pointed comment to the 'All Together' services. He says:

'I'll admit it. My initial reaction wasn't one of spontaneous enthusiasm. Definitely no cartwheels. I'm not particularly over-sensitive about being male, in my mid-thirties and still single, but the prospect of the introduction of regular "all-age" services at St Bill's had me thinking that maybe now was the time to head off for the Trappist monastery!

'As far as I was concerned "all-age" was just another way of saying "family worship". Nothing wrong with that at all. It's just that for many single people, the word "family", especially in a church context, has an amazing ability to press the paranoia button. It's great to emphasise family values and, of course, the local church should try to support parents in the tough task of bringing up their children. It's just that, in my experience, the more stress a church puts on being "family-based", the more likely it is that people who don't fit into the conventional family mould will feel sidelined. And I don't just mean single people: "family first" thinking can affect childless couples, retired people and people living with disability just as much. For a surprisingly high proportion of Christians, I'd guess that the word "family" gives a message that's as unmistakable as it is unintentional: "You are not included."

'So, as you might imagine, when "All Together" was proposed, I was not brimming with optimism. It looked like having all the hallmarks of everything I find most trying on a Sunday morning, what I call the "Triple C Factor" – choruses, children and chaos. But, I reckoned, if anyone could make a success of it, it would be Alf and Lizzie. And anyway, whether I liked it or not, I was already involved. In a moment of weakness, I'd allowed Lizzie to persuade me to draw some cartoons, both for publicity and as illustrations for talks, prayers and readings.

'We're a year into it now. Looking back to my initial fears and (yes, I'll admit it) to a certain amount of cynicism, I can see that I was both wrong *and* right.

'I was wrong to think that "All Together" would be a re-hash of the traditional family service formula of action songs, limp drama sketches and the kind of talk that aims to reach everyone, but only succeeds in communicating nothing very much to nobody in particular. I was also wrong to think it would be chaotic. True, it's often noisy, occasionally a little anarchic, but underpinning it there's a carefully thought-out structure.

'The Alternative Service Book meets Saturday morning television – if I was pushed, I guess that's how I'd describe "All Together". It's made up of seven or eight short segments. Some of the titles are descriptive (Green Scene, News Shot), others are zany (Hot Spot, Zingy Thingy) and some (Prayers and The Talk) are comfortingly traditional. I think many people are surprised to find that we use responsive prayers, have readings and say the Confession.

'More important, I think, is the fact that, whether the items are crazy or conventional, people *know what to expect and what is expected of them.* As a result they feel comfortable. The children know when they're expected to be noisy and spontaneous. They also know when they are expected to be quiet and receptive. Similarly, while some of the older folk may find the more hyperactive parts a little overpowering, they know roughly how long they are going to last and can therefore, as they say, adjust their dispositions accordingly.

'Certainly, as a single person I've not felt left out. In fact, what has impressed me most has been the wide spectrum of contributions that Alf and Liz have been able to draw from the congregation. More than simply discovering a few "hidden talents" (mind you, we are still talking about seventy-six-year-old Mr Thompson's tap-dance routine), we have been slowly finding out how much we all have to learn from each other, regardless of age or status.

'Backing it up, of course, has been some fairly serious planning, preparation and committed hard work. Alf and Lizzie have made a tremendous contribution. Together with Anne, our vicar, "All Together" was very much their "vision" for the church. Without their level of energy and infectious enthusiasm, I think it would have fallen flat – they prove the old showbiz maxim, "It's not what you do, it's the way that you do it." Another important contributory factor, I'm certain, has been the ongoing commitment of all our house groups to pray regularly for "All Together".

'Another positive by-product is that the church now looks a lot brighter. No major reordering, but it's amazing what a difference a few well-made, attractively coloured banners can make. Mind you, with people becoming more aware of the importance of visual impact, it won't be long before we're asking searching questions about sight-lines, visibility and lighting.

'And how was I right? I said I was worried that "All Together" would make us more of a "family-oriented" church. Well, it has. But not, I hastily add, in the way that I feared. Very gradually some of the fences we have erected between our cosy "nuclear" families are breaking down. I think we're beginning to catch a vision of the church as much more of an old-style "extended" family, a place where there's a positive role for *everybody*, not just mum, dad and the two point four. We've a long way to go, but I'm certain that "All Together" is helping us become a more "inclusive" community.

'And finally … I hate to admit it but, quietly and insistently, "All Together" has been chipping away at a few deeply held personal assumptions. Without realising it, I had been holding on to a very "me first" attitude to church in general, and to Sunday mornings in particular. When it came to assessing any innovation, my sole criterion was "What am *I* going to get out of it?" I was against anything that threatened the peace of my weekly "spiritual oasis".

'The "All Together" experience has taught me that there are vital lessons to be learned when the *whole* of God's people gets together – good things that simply aren't available when we stay in our conventional compartments. Of course, there's no way we're going to abandon all our other age-group oriented services and activities. I'm convinced that if St Will's is to be the body of Christ, then the sooner we all develop an "us first" attitude, the better. Somehow, I think the shift involved in making that change is going to be more revolutionary – for us and for our community – than we imagine.'

'Better Together'

Mary Bradshaw is Ben's and Kate's grandmother. With a lifetime's experience of every kind of church involvement, she and her husband John are, in their quiet way, a pillar of St William's. Mary says:

'I suppose John and I come in to the category of "Old Timers". We've been at St William's longer than most: we were married here, the children grew up here and now our grandchildren are regular attenders. Three vicars have come and gone in that time. We've seen plenty of changes – in the church and out in the community as well. Enough to make us more than a little cautious about innovation "just for the sake of it".

'When "All Together" began I thought, I hope this title isn't tempting providence. If we fail to live up to our claim of a Sunday morning that's genuinely for everyone, then pretty soon there'll be disgruntled folk calling it "Some Together" and we'll be worse off than when we started. In any case, all the different age groups are so *very* diverse in their interests nowadays. I wondered how *anyone* could come up with a formula that would appeal to everyone, from the tiny tots right up to me and John and all the other "oldies".

'Of course, it *is* an impossible task! I think part of the success

19

of "All Together" has been due to the fact that the leaders have recognised that fact right from the start. Rather than trying to make every bit of the service suit every single member of the congregation, they have tried to ensure that each week there are at least one or two items that will be meaningful to most. For instance, different groups of people lead the intercessions each week – you can't really expect the tinies to pay much attention to that. Similarly, much as John and I love to see Ben and his friends joining in so enthusiastically, we usually heave a quiet sigh of relief when some of the more outrageous parts of the service are over.

'I have to admit that I feared that all this emphasis on involving the youngsters was going to turn Sunday morning upside down. I was worried that the tail would end up wagging the dog, if you know what I mean. Fortunately that hasn't happened. Alf and Lizzie Burrows, for all their energy and enthusiasm, set high standards for the children. In fact, the way they control them reminds me of my long-ago teacher's "secret of success": "Be firm; be fair; be fun."

'One very practical measure has made a big difference as well – the "Happy Bags". These are small cloth bags that hang on pegs at the back of the church; the blue ones are for the very little children, the red ones for those a little older. Each bag contains a picture book, a toy, a puzzle – just enough to provide a little temporary, quiet distraction. They need someone to keep an eye on them, of course – my friend Mavis and I rejoice in the title of official "bag monitors"!

'What difference has "All Together" made to us at St William's? I can think of three developments which I think are important.

'The first is personal. John and I find that we can now talk more easily with the grandchildren about what happens in church, and about our faith as well. The things that happen in the new service give us some common ground. Ben, of course, is at the stage where he'll enthuse about anything that catches his interest. Kate, on the other hand, is very much at the "awkward age" and with teenage fashions (*those boots!*) and interests being so *very* different from times past, John and I feared that we were rapidly losing touch with her. Well, her clothes haven't changed (any colour, as long as it's black) but we now find that she'll chat very interestingly about her "green" concerns and we find that she's surprisingly well-informed on current affairs – hidden depths.

'Secondly, the new-style service has attracted quite a few newcomers. One such family usually sits near us – Jenny with her four children, all under six. David, her husband, is a policeman working shifts, so more often than not she is on her own with her very lively brood. I'm not sure how it has happened, but over the months John and I have got to know Jenny quite well and now the children seem to treat us as "surrogate grandparents". We're always happy to have one or two of them sit with us. We explain what's going on in the service, help them through the prayers and, when all else fails, there are always the Happy Bags to fall back on. I'll admit that in the past, I should probably have been far less friendly. In fact I can remember many occasions when I've sat in splendid isolation, staring stonily at similar young parents with squirming children. I've also noticed that we aren't the only "oldies" to take a similar interest in younger families. In fact, sometimes I wonder if it is we who are adopting them, or they who are adopting us – either way, I think it's rather a good thing.

'My third reason? Well, it may seem rather a strange one. "All Together" has involved making changes. I'll admit that there's much about the old-style Sunday mornings that both John and I miss. But, on reflection, we are both happier with the way things are going now. It has not been an easy ride – change always involves a certain amount of pain. But it's worth it. I think the clue lies in that word "together". John and I have been rereading Acts recently: it's all about the first Christians living, growing and working *together*. No signs of traditional British reserve for them – church life was based on mutual service, mutual self-giving.

'No, John and I have not decided to open our home as a commune. But we have been challenged by "All Together" to think of the church in quite a different way – a bit more about sharing, a bit less about individualism. In a way, it reminds me a little of the war – it's amazing what people can do, and *enjoy* doing, when everybody pitches in for the "good of the cause".'

Fundamental questions

Too good to be true? Very possibly. But what excites me about imaginary St William's isn't only the brass-tacks actuality of what they are doing in their 'All Together' services. Innovative and original as it is, there's something even more revolutionary going on behind their activity. As well as doing, they are *thinking*.

My hope for this book is that it will stimulate thought *and* encourage action. The men, women and children of St Will's are asking some fundamental questions about the church – they are the questions which I want to address in this book. How we answer them could make a radical difference to how we live out our Christian faith at the dawn of the new century.

The difficult definition – what do we mean by 'family'?

Most agree that these are troubled times for families. Increasing numbers of marriages end in divorce; many children grow up in single-parent households; more and more couples choose to live together without the traditional commitment of marriage. But, at the same time, TV and newspaper advertising continues to portray families as squeaky-clean units of middle-class mum, dad and no more than two happy children. Our politicians (whatever the state of their private lives) urge us to get 'back to basics' and return to 'traditional family values'. Throughout all the discussion there seems to be a silent agreement that we all know what we mean when we talk about the 'family'. Even if we can't define the word exactly, at least we agree that, like 'mom and apple pie', it must be a good thing.

I, for one, am not at all sure that we do know what we mean. I'm convinced that the church urgently needs to examine its current range of definitions of the word 'family'. Where do they come from? How well do they stand up in comparison with biblical patterns of community life? Just what are we trying to say when we advertise our fellowship as a 'family church'?

I can't quite place you – how do children fit in to the church?

If our churches are confused about the meaning of 'family', it is hardly surprising that there are so many inconsistencies in the way we treat our children. What is their true status? How should we value them? Are they an 'extra' on the agenda of church life, or should they be playing an important role alongside the adult fellow-Christians in the development of the kingdom?

Body language – what do we mean when we say 'church'?

Start asking questions and more questions follow. Examining how children fit into the church will inevitably lead to asking how all of us fit into the extraordinary new community that the Holy Spirit set in motion at the first Pentecost. I'm excited by the growing number of Christians who are rediscovering what it means to be Christ's church in their local community. It's a process which makes a huge difference to what happens on Sundays – but it also has a transforming effect on the rest of the week as well.

Community values – how should we relate to each other in the church?

At fictional St William's, ordinary people were finding that making Sunday worship more inclusive has important 'knock on' effects. Barriers start to fall, those who were on the margin move nearer the centre and people discover new ways of serving, and being served by, each other.

The great infiltration – just where do our values come from?

I want to encourage people to think – and think hard – about what we do and why we do it. We pay lip service to living by biblical principles, but how much of our current practice would pass the test of being put through the 'scriptural filter'? How much would turn out to be influenced predominantly by the values and assumptions of our contemporary culture?

Whole in one – how do I balance 'my needs' with 'our needs'?

I've noticed recently that there's a word that seems to be frequently on the lips of some of my Christian friends – 'spirituality'. Many are rediscovering new approaches to prayer, new avenues for developing their personal relationship with God, new and creative ways of enhancing their journey of faith. There's a growing popularity for retreats. I know many people who come back restored and refreshed from a week on the island of Iona, or in the international community at Taizé. I'm all in favour – well, almost all in favour.

Pursuing an individual spirituality is fine as long as it doesn't reinforce a 'me first' attitude to the church. I'm certain that for too long we have allowed ourselves to be influenced by secular society's conviction that 'self-development' should be high on everybody's agenda. The church was never intended to be a 'me first' place.

Paul urged his friends in Ephesus: 'Submit to one another out of reverence for Christ' (Ephesians 5:21). My hope for this book is that the reader will be able to share, and 'catch', a vision for the church as a network of mutually submitted relationships between Christians of *all* ages, a day-to-day working out of what happens when we say, 'I'm not here for me. I'm here for you.'

CHAPTER TWO

A BIBLICAL VIEW OF FAMILY AND CHILDREN

Family. What pictures does the word conjure up? How many people do you see in your mind's eye? Mum, Dad and two or three children enjoying a day out? Or maybe a larger gathering of grandparents, aunts, uncles, cousins and in-laws at Christmas or at a wedding. For many, of course, it is a much smaller unit.

It is likely that your idea of a 'normal' family will depend very much on your background and your expectations. Your nationality will probably be an important influence as well. Accept an invitation to 'meet the family' in Kent and you will probably be introduced, at most, to half a dozen people; in Kenya, you might meet the whole village.

Flick through the pages of a glossy magazine, or watch a few commercial breaks on the television and you'll be left in no doubt about our society's ideal of the family: a prosperous, cosy unit of two healthy, happy parents, two (or possibly three) healthy, happy children and, of course, a puppy. When it comes to the family, we are not encouraged to think big – or to think realistically. The 'fantasy families' of the advertisements bear scant resemblance to life as it is lived for many of today's growing number of single parents.

Bombarded as we are with images of the compact 'nuclear' family, it's easy to forget that it is only relatively recently that we have come to believe that small is normal. On the whole, the communities our great-grandparents grew up in were more settled and less mobile than those of our fast-paced, end-of-century world. Families were larger, child-care was often shared across a network of family members and, on the whole, elderly parents were looked after in the home. The children of seventy years ago grew up relating naturally to far more adults than just their parents. It's easy to see that how we think of the family will be a major influence on how we think of children.

The child in the Old Testament

Interestingly, the Bible doesn't have a word that's equivalent to our modern idea of family. In the Old Testament world, children grew up in a 'household' which may have included many people. The smallest recognised family unit consisted of three to four generations living in neighbouring houses. Membership of the household did not depend exclusively on blood relationships: servants were as much a part of the household as anyone else. This extended family was linked to the larger grouping of the clan, which in turn was a member of the even bigger unit – the tribe.

In ancient Israel children were neither unimportant nor insignificant. Rather they were 'hidden' within the strong kinship bonds which held the Old Testament peoples together. They were brought up among a large group of adult relatives, rather than relating mainly to their parents, as in the contemporary Western pattern.

Shared responsibility

Did this mean that in Old Testament times the bond between parent and child was not taken very seriously? Far from it! What it did mean was that children did not depend solely on mother and father for all of their guidance, nurture and discipline. There was a pool of skills and experience from which they could draw. However busy your parents may have been, there was always grandmother to go to for a story, an uncle to teach you how to make a clay pot, an aunt to sort out a quarrel or a cousin who needed help with his flock. In terms of child-care alone, it was a way of life that had many advantages.

Shared experience

The Old Testament is the story of a community. The Jewish people believed that God had chosen them, spoken to them and dealt with them as a community. At the heart of their experience of God was their shared memory of how he had miraculously intervened in their history by rescuing them from slavery in Egypt and leading them to their own homeland.

Wrapped up in that story were the answers to two profound questions: 'Who is God?' and 'Who are we?' Fail to remember that story and you might as well forget about being a Jew, forget about God and forget about being a nation.

And how were you supposed to make sure that your children learned this vital lesson? Send them to school? Give them a book? Wait until they were old enough to find out for themselves? No, instead simply share the story regularly with the children at a special household meal; make it fun; allow them to join in so that they become part of the story and, eventually, the story becomes part of them. The Passover meal was for the whole family. Children had a central role in it. They were participants, not spectators. And while it is true that formal education became increasingly important throughout the later part of the Old Testament period, the heart of every child's training was in the home.

Shared welfare

The Jewish community was about more than education. The combination of household, tribe and clan made an effective welfare system. It provided protection for both individuals and families and was actively concerned for their good. Each tribe had varying degrees of responsibilities and rights concerning the guarding and upholding of this welfare system.

God can choose children too

I find the story of the young Samuel particularly interesting and important. Here is a child with a strongly developed relationship with God and who is most definitely a participant, not just an observer.

From the story it is clear that Samuel's acceptance into service with Eli wasn't questioned, despite his 'tender' years. At each stage of their relationship God deals with Samuel in a way that is appropriate to the boy's age. God speaks directly *to* Samuel. God speaks *through* Samuel to his people.

The Old Testament takes a very open attitude to the spiritual significance and contribution of children. They can both hear and receive God's words and on certain occasions they can speak them out to God's people.

Serious business

Another interesting glimpse into God's heart for children comes in the final verses of the Old Testament. Reminding the people of the fundamental importance of their covenant relationship with God, Malachi writes:

> See, I will send you the prophet Elijah before that great and dreadful

The benefits of the system weren't just for those within the community. Take a look at the story of Ruth to see how the system took account of the most vulnerable of outsiders – a widowed refugee with a dependent mother-in-law.

So important were kinship relationships that it was this network of obligations and mutual support, rather than the parent-child relationship, that bound the Jewish tribe together. Obviously, any breakdown in the system affected the whole tribe in general, and its most vulnerable members in particular: widows, orphans, the elderly, the infirm.

Breakdown of kinship relationships spelled tragedy for household, clan and tribe – socially, spiritually and day of the Lord comes. He will turn the hearts of the fathers to their children, and the hearts of the children to their fathers; or else I will come and strike the land with a curse.'

(Malachi 4: 5-6)

The relationship between the children and their earthly fathers is viewed as God-given. It is something holy – holy in the sense that God ordained his people to live in a special way, set apart from the pattern of life of other nations.

The relationship of parent to child is a reflection of God's relationship to the nation – provider, carer, protector, wise judge and spiritual teacher. And it was through the outworking of this relationship that God's people were able to become what he intended them to be – a light to the nations.

What a commission that was for those fathers about whom Malachi wrote! They were to disregard it at their peril: accompanying the promise of blessing is a warning of a curse. Anyone interfering with what had been vowed by God – in this case the nurture and care of the children – could expect severe discipline. The whole nation – not just the clan or local grouping of believers, but the whole family of God – had vowed to keep, guard and nurture this relationship between the children and their fathers.

economically. When King Ahab took a fancy to Naboth's vineyard (1 Kings 21) he was doing more than starting a business dispute about property. He was destroying a whole family. This and many other Old Testament passages (Micah 2:1-5; Isaiah 5:8; Nehemiah 5) demonstrate that a threat to the kinship relationships that nurtured, protected and provided for families was considered a social evil – something abhorred by God and which was to be severely punished.

Shared learning, shared worship

The Jewish people could never take their relationship with God for granted. If the nation was to survive, the bond between men, women and children and their Creator had to be constantly renewed. Before entering the land of promise, Moses emphasised that this was more than a matter of individual study or piety. It was to be a community activity:

> Assemble the people – men, women and children, and the aliens living in your towns – so that they can listen and learn to fear the Lord your God and follow carefully all the words of this law.
>
> (Deuteronomy 31:12)

Celebration, too, involved everyone, regardless of age or status:

> Be joyful at your feast – you, your sons and daughters, your menservants and maidservants, and the Levites, the aliens, the fatherless and the widows who live in your towns.
>
> (Deuteronomy 16:14)

The inclusion of children is so much part and parcel of the Old Testament attitude to life, that it's easy to overlook it. But again and again, when God's people were praying, learning, sacrificing, worshipping, mourning or rejoicing, their children were there with them, at the heart of the community.

Then and now

Even if we wanted to, we couldn't recreate the conditions in which those long-ago extended families lived and thrived. Theirs was a world of crops, herds and crafts – ours one of computers, cars and consumerism. Their lives were governed by the seasons, ours by all the complex demands of a high-tech industrial society. Like it or not, a chasm of centuries separates our world from that of the Old Testament.

But despite the differences, I'm convinced that when we look at the principles underlying family life in ancient Israel we can discover some powerfully challenging parallels for today.

Safety in numbers

Life was harsh. Crops had a habit of failing; disease might strike the herds; there was the ever-present threat of attack by hostile neighbours. There was safety in numbers, and it made sense for families to be large, co-operative and cohesive.

This extended family was able to meet most of the basic needs of its members: child-care, education, employment, health and provision for old age. When it came to looking after the whole person, the Old Testament family makes a startling model of 'care in the community'.

Yet while the family's social function was important, it was only a reflection of fundamental spiritual values shared by the whole nation. They were God's covenant people, called into special relationship with him. But the 'vertical' relationship with the Creator meant nothing if it was not worked out horizontally within the community. And the community was the context in which God expected his people to grow in knowledge of him, to praise and worship him and to teach their children about him.

Along with adolescents, adults and the elderly, the children were welcomed, acknowledged and cared for. Their needs didn't take priority, but neither were they ignored. And while the rights and responsibilities of parents were upheld, the whole community took a supporting role in the nurture of its younger members. It was a community without compartments.

What about us?

The coming of Jesus, the Messiah, began a new covenant between God and his people. It changed everything. Before, Israel was like a tree whose growth depended on the constant support and tending provided by the Law. Christ's death and resurrection began a completely new phase of growth; instead of external support, the new covenant community, the church, would grow and flourish because it had the life and power of God *within* it. But it's important to remember that though the life is new, the tree is the same. That is why the church can never throw away the Old Testament; freed by grace from the 'life support system' of the Law, we still inherit its promises and principles. As the apostle Paul expressed it: 'Now that faith has come, we are no longer under the supervision of the law,' (Galatians 3:25). The church is now the people of God, the new covenant people. And those churches which baptise infants believe that baptism takes the place of circumcision as the sign of belonging to God's people.

Care, sharing, co-operation, mutual protection, inclusiveness – these are the qualities that made the Old Testament family special. Surely the same qualities should be the mark of each and every local church today?

I believe our churches and congregations are like aspects of those ancient 'kinship' groups, and similarly want to care for, guard and uphold family life. Being the body of Christ is about interdependence, and I am certain that anything that threatens our commitment to nurturing all ages in God's family is a serious threat to the well-being of the church today.

Caring deeply about community is likely to cause conflict. Increasingly throughout this century, we have been encouraged to be individualistic. On the whole, we think that happiness in life comes as a result of self-discovery and self-improvement. It's a trend that truly found its stride in the boom years of the 1980s, when suddenly it seemed (at least for the high-fliers) that there were no limits to the benefits to be reaped from our 'enterprise culture'. Nothing could be further from the Old Testament model of kinship and kinship values, which was corporate, just, giving and sharing.

I believe that it is in this context of a rediscovery of a biblical view of family and community that the church has to work out how it should value, protect, nurture and encourage the children in its midst. As we rediscover our responsibility towards each other, I am certain we shall catch a new vision of God's concern for the spiritual and physical welfare of our children.

Family – deciding what we mean

'Welcome to our church family' – it's something we often say. And though I'm not doubting the sincerity of the greeting, a lot depends on what we mean by that word 'family'. Travelling around a great many churches in recent years, and meeting many people in the process, I find that 'family' is definitely a 'hot' word: one that nearly always sparks a reaction, often a negative one.

Churches use the word with the best of intentions, but often it backfires on them. What could be more inclusive than advertising your fellowship as a 'family church'? Sadly, for many this can have the opposite effect, giving them a painful feeling of exclusion. Men and women who are widowed, divorced or separated, who are lone parents or who have never been married, are keenly aware of the ways in which their day-to-day experience differs from the cosy perfection of the families in the TV commercials. For them the word 'family' gives a very clear message: 'Not you!'

Plenty of churches, of course, recognise the problem and organise a variety of groups and meetings to help meet a wide range of needs. We regularly get together as older people or as young mums, as singles or marrieds, as toddlers or teenagers. The aim – and it's very commendable – is that nobody should feel left out. But often, I feel, in our enthusiasm to make everybody feel included, we run a serious risk – the danger of fragmenting our fellowships into a variety of independent 'interest groups'.

We have learned much in recent years about caring and sharing in small groups. In our fast-moving, anonymous world, they have become fertile oases of Bible study, prayer, worship, mutual support and encouragement. There's no doubt that the 'small groups movement' has made a huge contribution to the life of the church. But I wonder if, in the process, we haven't been neglecting to relate to each other in the context of the larger congregation. Being the church on the 'micro' level of small groups and meetings is fine – but not if we ignore the challenge to be the body of Christ on the 'macro' scale as well.

The church is in the business of proposing alternative views.

As we have seen, the Old Testament picture of the family offers an exciting challenge to our society's pared-down packages of parents and children all living in isolation from each other. There's nothing wrong with a church having a flourishing small-group programme. But I'm convinced that we need to be equally concerned to relate to one another *as a community* as we worship God on Sundays. Being the church is about listening to God *together*, about learning to be vulnerable to him and to each other *together* – and it is about doing those things as a family, as God's household, right across the generations.

Where are you now?

What practical steps can we take to start encouraging the values of caring and interdependence that made the Old Testament family so strong and so distinctive? These questions and activities may stimulate discussion:

- Ask people to give a brief, off-the-cuff definition of the word 'family'. Then discuss the pictures that emerge. Compare them with the Old Testament extended 'household' and with our modern stereotypes of family life.
- Where does our idea of 'family' come from? How much have we as the church, nationally and locally, 'bought into' the present set of cultural values without realising it?
- To what extent does the concept of 'kinship' interdependence operate in your church, especially with reference to the nurture and protection of children?
- Who has the responsibility for the welfare and nurture of children and family life in your church? Is this concern on the Church Council/Meeting agenda?
- Does your church have any plans for a teaching programme about family life? (For example, *HELP! I'm a parent*, a video-based resource from the Church Pastoral Aid Society.)
- How does your church support families facing difficult circumstances? What provision is there for single parents,

those caring for elderly and infirm parents, those dealing with long- or short-term physical, mental or behavioural problems with their children?

● Do you pray for the children of your friends and acquaintances and the children in your church family?

● What could you be doing to contribute to building better relationships across the age groups in your church?

The child in the New Testament

Challenging attitudes

Jesus had a very strange attitude to children. At least that's what the religious leaders of first-century Palestine thought. For a start, the fact that he actually *had an attitude* was worrying enough; he did more than merely teach them, he *actively engaged* with them as well. He spoke to them; he spoke about them; he healed them. He even raised them from the dead. All this, combined with the way he treated women, was enough to persuade the Pharisees that here was a potentially dangerous radical.

It was therefore quite a natural reaction from the disciples when they tried to keep children out of Jesus' way and 'ticked off' eager parents (or possibly older brothers and sisters) when they tried to bring children to be blessed by Jesus.

Recognising need

In Matthew 15:22-28 a Canaanite mother begs Jesus to have mercy on her and her suffering daughter. Jesus had made it clear that his main mission was to the Jews, and the disciples had wanted to send the woman away. Jesus, however, recognises the mother's longing and faith. He heals her daughter.

The crowd of eager parents had already witnessed or heard about similar miracles. They are natural opportunists, eager that their children shall not miss out. Jesus doesn't appear to mind their mixed motives for coming, because his main focus is on the children: 'Let [permit, allow] the little children to come to me'

Food for thought

We often talk and pray about living like Jesus. Most of us will readily admit that we desire to bear his character, to become more like him. But I wonder how many of us have paused to read, study and consider the implications of the passages of Scripture involving Jesus with children. How many of us have consciously modelled our behaviour, attitude and actions towards children on these passages, which describe to vividly Jesus' welcoming attitude towards them?

I was challenged by this poem by Nigel Forde:

> *A church should feed the spirit and the mind*
> *Of every taste, sex, age, that makes mankind;*
> *None should be left out or left behind*
> *(And if one is, will it be Major Thrales*
> *or young Ben Brown with dirty nails?).*
> *Or is church just a useful apparatus*
> *To sort us out according to our status?*
> *As if the sidesman were to hear a knock*
> *At the west door and opening it, take stock:*
> *'Horn-rimmed specs, bank balance, safe career?*
> *Come in! Come in! We think you'll like it here!'*
> *But eight year old or toddler? Or just*
> *A babe-in-arms? 'Well come in … if you must!'*
>
> ('Video Poem', *Children in the Way* video,
> Church of England Board of Education, 1988)

(Matthew 19:14). Jesus emphasises this point by forbidding the disciples to hinder the children coming.

Word and action

Have you noticed that the descriptions of Jesus' encounters with children always record actions as well as words? They show him *doing* as well as *saying*. Jesus engages practically and physically with the person and the situation. He takes the girl's hand and speaks to her. He takes children in his arms and blesses them. He places a child in the midst of his disciples, displaying tenderness, compassion, welcome and acceptance through his actions.

The New Testament challenges us to welcome, accept and 'engage with' children. It warns us about using their tender years as an excuse for discriminating against them because, as Jesus indicated, they have a special place in the kingdom.

Children in the kingdom

Jesus said: 'Whoever humbles himself like this child is the greatest in the kingdom of heaven' (Matthew 18:4); 'Whoever welcomes one of these little children in my name welcomes me' (Mark 9:36-37). Jesus regarded the children as *already* belonging to the kingdom. For adults his call was to repent, believe and follow him. He spoke of some adults as 'not far from the kingdom' (Mark 12:34). Others he spoke of as needing to 'enter the kingdom' (Matthew 18:3). But of children Jesus says: 'the kingdom of heaven belongs to such as these' (Matthew 19:14).

Scholars may differ in their interpretation of this verse, some arguing that Jesus is not referring directly to children, but to those who are *like* children. I disagree. I cannot understand how it is possible to exclude children from this important 'kingdom statement'. How can we ignore the presence of children when Jesus is described as taking them in his arms and blessing them? I believe this is directly about children, *as well as* about those who are like children.

A question of status

Our actions are governed by our beliefs. Everything we do, or fail to do, for children and young people will be affected by our understanding, conscious or unconscious, of their standing before God. Are the children of Christian parents outside the kingdom until they come to a conscious personal acceptance of Jesus as Lord and Saviour? (If that is the case, then what is the significance of infant baptism?) Or are they inside until they consciously 'opt out'?

I am convinced that the children of believing parents are Christians too – fellow-pilgrims with us on the journey of faith. I believe that we need to wake up to the implications of their status as such. Like all members of the church, they can both receive and offer ministry, in proportion to their emerging gifts and abilities. Jesus welcomed children not merely for their potential for the future, but also for their 'here and now' importance. As the book *Children in the Way* comments, Jesus saw them not simply as 'objects of education, those who need to be brought and trained for adulthood before they achieve any real significance. Rather [he saw them as] patterns of discipleship, those who teach as well as learn' (*Children in the Way*, Ed. Turk, Church House Publishing, 1988, p74).

Of course, it is true that quite young children may respond to the 'call' of Jesus. My own husband came to Christ at a Crusader class when he was eight years old. But what about the under sevens, the infants? While I believe God's Spirit can reach and touch the youngest child, how can that child be expected to respond in a conscious way? God always deals with us with respect to our age and stage of faith.

Therefore it would seem entirely consistent to me, if a baby who is entirely dependent on his or her father and mother's love and provision is viewed by God as *already* in a dependent and loving relationship with him as his or her heavenly Father.

Speaking for myself, I believe *all* young children are to be regarded as Christ's. But because they are dependent on the lifestyle of their parents, they may grow up to reject him, if their parents do not have a living faith and if Christ is not being made 'real' to them in other situations, places and relationships.

Believing parents need to *bring* their children to Christ. Their responsibility is to help their children grow into a conscious relationship with Jesus in the context of the family, both at home and at church. It is also their duty to do all they can to ensure that their children remain *in* the kingdom. And, of course, it is vitally important that parents and leaders of children's work know what

---

Thought-provoking quotes

It is because the kingdom of God is theirs that they are to come to Jesus ... the child is invited to Jesus because the kingdom is already granted to him/her.

(John Pridmore, 'All God's Children',
Third Way magazine, 1978)

Jesus refers to the actual children which were brought to him. Because the original Aramaic must have said: 'To these and other such children belongs the kingdom of God.'

(Hans Ruedi Weber, *Jesus and the Children*,
World Council of Churches, 1979)

Surely the truth is that all children are included in the great atoning sacrifice and belong to Jesus Christ until they deliberately refuse him.

(Dr Griffith Thomas, *Principles of Theology*, Article 27)

---

they believe about their children's relationship with God and also what will best build, maintain and bring growth to that relationship.

All together

Right from the start Christians met in the homes of fellow believers (Acts 1:13; 2:46; 5:42; 12:12). The household gathering was the basic unit of the early church. Because they met in homes, women were able to participate and children were included. Previously, women's roles had been subordinate ones, but the New Testament consistently portrays women as being involved in the life and ministry of the church (Galatians 3:28; Colossians 3:11). Scriptural and historical evidence suggests that children were present as *participants* in these early Christian household gatherings.

In his book, *Going to Church in the First Century*, Robert Banks paints a picture of what it may have been like to attend an early Christian gathering. He begins with the arrival of a variety of people, including a large family, consisting of parents, four children and an elderly grandmother. The children are welcomed and are obviously comfortable with their surroundings. Adults, children and slaves gather around the common table and take part in the meal, which, with its sharing of bread and wine, is the focal point of their worship.

As the meal ends and it gets dark, the children play games with one of the adults, while the other adults continue their conversations. Children are clearly allowed to behave as children and adults as adults. The general atmosphere is one of people being comfortable with one another. Later he describes how they pray and worship together and how men, women *and* children participate. As the evening deepens and the children grow sleepy, the gathering hears from one or two gifted teachers and then people minister to one another before leaving around curfew time. The children are present throughout the fellowship time – the breaking of bread, worship, prayer, teaching, exhortation, exercise of spiritual gifts and ministry.

The picture – and of course it is only a picture – is one of inclusion. As John Pridmore writes: 'The child belonged to his family; if the family belonged to the church, then so did the child.'

The New Testament gives us many insights into God's relationship with children – and into the relationship between children and their parents. Writing to the Christians at Ephesus, Paul addresses different groups, among them the children. He charges them to 'obey your parents in the Lord' (Ephesians 6:1). He goes on to remind them of the Old Testament promise linked to the fifth commandment: 'that it may go well with you in the land that the Lord your God is giving you' (Deuteronomy 5:16). It is interesting to notice that Paul addresses the children directly; he writes with the assumption that they are responsible members of the community.

I'm convinced from my reading of the New Testament and my

studies of the early communities of the Christian church that the upbringing and nurture of children in Christian families was the responsibility of the whole household gathering. John Pridmore comments: 'For the youngest child, his family is his church; all he can know of God is mediated through his family. The role of the wide church is to support and assist the fellowship of the "church in the house".'

Local or universal?

Finally, if we are to understand how children fit in to the local church, it's vital to have a firm grasp of what we mean by the universal church which Jesus founded. It is not a club, a friendly society or a social work agency – though, of course, it may at times function like any of them. As I noted earlier, it is far more than any of those. Christians share the astonishing privilege of belonging to the community of the new covenant between the Creator and his creatures. Membership is based solely on what Christ achieved for us by his death and resurrection. The New Testament recognised a simple, threefold process of initiation involving faith, repentance and baptism. And though scholars disagree about exactly when the baptism of infants began, the Scriptures make it clear that following conversion, the whole household was recognised as being fully inside the covenant community.

Both Old and New Testaments picture children growing up in a variety of family situations, most of them large-scale, all of them covering several generations. To experience family life was to experience community. When Jesus founded his church he called everybody into a renewed experience of community. In the church we never stop being individuals, but if we are to be the community God intends us to be, we have to learn to let go of some of our twentieth-century *individualistic* attitudes.

Bible Focus

Here is an outline for study and discussion based on Matthew 18:1-5.

1. Jesus calls a little child to stand in the middle of the group of disciples. Then Jesus addresses them: 'I tell you the truth, unless you change and become like little children, you will never enter the kingdom of heaven' (verse 3).

In *Matthew for Today* (Hodder & Stoughton, 1988), Michael Green comments:

> The phrase 'little ones' recurs in verses 10 and 14 and it seems to be used ambivalently to denote both the little child and 'little people', those whom people regard as insignificant, but on whom God looks in a very different light. The church should be a place where both are honoured. Children matter. They mattered to Jesus. They matter in any congregation. The services should be arranged with their needs in view. They need to be befriended, understood and taught. The way we behave to children is one of the indicators of the way we behave to Jesus. That is quite a thought!

● What questions and issues does this raise for you?
● What do you think Jesus meant by the phrase, 'Unless you change and become like little children' (verse 3)? (The word 'change' here does not indicate a need to return to a state of childhood, but rather a change of direction and behaviour. In this context, the word means the alteration of the whole way the disciples, and those to whom Matthew was writing, viewed children's status in the kingdom of heaven.)

2. Jesus then presents his criterion for judging who has important status in the kingdom of heaven:

'Whoever humbles himself like this child is the greatest in the kingdom of heaven' (verse 4).

● What status do you think the church has given children?

● Do you agree with Michael Green when he says that the church should be a place where children matter and where they are honoured?
● If you do agree, how is this planned for, worked out and achieved in your church?

3. 'Whoever welcomes a little child like this in my name welcomes me' (verse 5). The way we receive and respond to children is an indication of how we receive Jesus and respond to him.

● If you believe that children should be welcomed among us, how should that welcome be expressed?

The early Christians referred to themselves as God's children. The believers were also referred to as 'the little ones'. Therefore many interpret this verse as Matthew addressing young Christians and challenging the churches to be more welcoming in fellowship and hospitality.

Other commentators say that the metaphor of the child points us to our position of grace (i.e. unearned status), suggesting that what Matthew is saying in chapter 18 is that the kingdom of God belongs to children and to those who make themselves vulnerable to God's grace, giving up status and importance, taking on the dependent role of the servant. It seems to me that both interpretations of this verse are valid, and are not mutually contradictory.

● What conclusions have you come to about the interpretations of these verses? Have you been challenged about how you view children?
● Is there anything you would like to change in the church, regarding how we welcome and respect children?
● Is there anything you would like to address, pray about or confront in yourself about how welcoming, receiving and honouring of children you are?

Summary

So what conclusions can we draw from looking at children in both the Old and New Testaments?

- Children are significant and of value to God.
- The relationship between parents and children needs to be rightly ordered.
- The children are nurtured in the context of the wider church family.
- The children are present with the adults at the main worship events.
- The children are welcomed, received and attended to as participants.
- The children are the responsibility of the whole extended family or household (Old Testament) or church gathering (New Testament).
- The children are *in* the kingdom until they 'opt out' rather than *outside* the kingdom until they 'opt in'.
- God's relationship with children in the Old and New Testaments is one of *fundamental acceptance.*

Children are significant, valued and most definitely *in* rather than outside the kingdom. God makes it clear that, in order to support this, he requires action from both parents and the 'household' of the church. He requires children to be nurtured, not only by the parents, but by the whole body of believers. He expects parents to 'rightly order' their family life, so that their children learn and experience the teaching and values of the kingdom. He requires the whole body of believers to welcome, receive and nurture the children as *full participants* in the kingdom.

These questions should help you focus:

- What is the 'theology of the child' in your church? Have you thought through the implications of your understanding of children's place and status within the kingdom of God?

- Are children to be regarded as being *in* the kingdom until they 'opt out' or *outside* the kingdom until they 'opt in'?
- What in your experience has most encouraged and 'built' faith in your children?

Children in today's culture

'Kids today! Just who do they think they are?' It's a familiar enough response to some of the headlines we've been reading recently. But if it is ever to be anything more than an outburst of adult frustration, I think there's another question that needs to be addressed first: 'Kids today! Just who do *we* think they are?'

If we are serious about making links between Old and New Testament principles and the needs of today's families, we should be thinking through some key issues about our children. What is their role in the modern world? How do we value them? What do we expect of them? Our answers to these questions (or lack of them) will have a direct bearing on how we welcome children into our churches.

Personally significant?

In modern Western culture children are generally viewed as being significant in their own right. They matter for themselves, not merely because they are someone's son or daughter. Also their value is based on who they are *now*, not on the fact that they are 'adults in the making', or 'wage-earners in waiting'.

Compared with the days when they were to be seen but not heard, we now have a much more welcoming and inclusive attitude to children. We place a high value on education and, increasingly, we want children to feel that they have a voice in what happens to them at school and college. And, though it remains a controversial area, our courts recognise that children have rights which must be protected.

Players or pawns?

But it's in the area of economics, in the developed West at least,

Valued or Victims?

Whether we like it or not (or even whether we admit or not) we are all hugely influenced by the modern mass media. Unless you're a hermit, it's impossible not to have your thinking, priorities and values affected by the daily avalanche of images and sound-bites from television, radio and newspapers. Some are good. Many are dreadful.

Adults are able to ignore or 'filter out' much of the dross. Children start without that advantage. It's something all thoughtful parents worry about, but few have the time or determination to monitor everything their children see. And children see a lot more than many parents realise. Primary school teachers know that many under-teens are regularly viewing videos which, a decade ago, would only have been seen by over-eighteen cinema audiences.

But however carefully you control what they see, there's no keeping contemporary influences completely at bay. For instance, this week my fourteen-year-old daughter's magazine carries an advertisement for a computer game called *Street Fighter*. The essence of this hugely popular 'martial arts' game is that the player sets up fights between various sets of nasty characters from around the world, using specialist moves like the 'hundred hand slap'! Harmless stuff, you might say, but what values are being drip-fed to our children as they spend hours of their free time absorbed in a gruesomely violent fantasy world?

that the status of children has changed most dramatically. Young interests and enthusiasms drive a multi-million dollar electronics and entertainment industry. The success of more companies than Nintendo and Sega depends on keeping a finger constantly on the pulse of children's current crazes.

Magazine publishers, toy manufacturers and fast-food chains compete fiercely for 'young money'. Switch on your television and check out the late afternoon soaps or Saturday morning magazine programmes. Second for second, the production costs of the commercials far exceed those of the programmes they interrupt. With amazing energy and creativity advertisers reflect and feed

The success of video games is based on the fact that they are strongly compulsive (particularly, it seems, for boys). Playing most of them is a solo activity. Unlike old-fashioned board games, there's no interaction with other people. No wonder teachers find it increasingly difficult to introduce children to co-operative play.

Some research suggests that there is a correlation between the regular, protracted viewing of violent computer games and videos and the increase of violence and bullying in schools. I am sure that videos are not the only factor in the increase of violence involving children. But I am concerned that we should hear and understand the warnings about what values our children are being fed through the constant images of violence (sometimes sexual) and destruction they are seeing on their computer screens, as well as on videos and television.

We live in a 'media age'. It offers our children an amazing, multi-coloured box of delights, full of much that is stimulating and challenging. Or, alternatively, it has given them a Pandora's box, releasing negative forces that threaten to turn them into a generation of self-centred, screen-addicted 'couch potatoes'. Probably the truth lies somewhere in the middle. At any rate, as the century ends and the next wave of the 'information revolution' accelerates, we will realise that what we are seeing now is only the very beginning of a profound change in the way we all live.

the desires of young consumers. Nobody knows better the relentless strength of a five-year-old's 'I want' or a teenager's 'Must have'. Naturally enough, the advertisers have a name for it: 'pester power'.

Televisions, videos, record players, personal computers – expensive items which were once 'one per household' are now standard equipment in many children's bedrooms. Why are parents willing to part with so much money? Many persuade themselves that these high-tech items (along with mountain bikes and Reebok trainers) are 'love offerings', proof of their determination to give their children the best of everything. Many of them are useful and educational – the buzz word is 'edutainment' – but aren't they also sometimes 'guilt-soothers', electronic child-minders to occupy the children while mother or father is busy elsewhere?

Me or us?

It's not only computer games and videos which threaten the old-fashioned notion that family life is about doing things *together*. Over recent years it seems to me that many well-intentioned parents, myself included, have been smitten with what I call 'club-mania' – the compulsion to keep our children continuously occupied outside the home.

My eleven-year-old has a very full diary. As well as three school clubs, she goes to Guides and various other clubs. She's also keen to go to ballet lessons. I've almost run out of days in the week. She has a great time, learns useful skills and makes friends. As I chauffeur her between activities, surely I'd be justified in feeling a mild glow of pride – after all, look at all the wonderful experiences I'm giving her. So why, then, do I have a distinct sense of unease?

I think it links back to what I said earlier about families. Most of us have to manage without the supportive network of the extended family. We yearn to give our children some of the richness of that experience. Sadly, too, we are painfully aware of how much the world has become a less safe place for children. To compensate, we look to a variety of outside agencies, clubs and classes. Though they are all good in themselves, it's their cumulative effect that worries me. We have to weigh our desire to encourage, challenge and inspire our children against the cost of the constant rushing of them from one activity to the next. It's vital to guard against the subtle undermining of our own personal 'quality time' with our children.

I recently met a dad in Scarborough, who talked about the importance in families of time together and family 'rituals' (things we do together that have particular and regular significance, e.g. decorating the Christmas tree together on Christmas eve).

This dad spoke of his own family ritual of baking a cake together in which all family members (even the youngest) had a contribution to make. Then on Sunday, they gave thanks, shared in a prayer time, and enjoyed eating the cake together.

This sort of family ritual requires some forethought, spiritual and practical, some planning and most importantly commitment from family members – but I believe it could be very valuable to us, both creatively and spiritually, in our busy twentieth century lives.

Double standards

As a society we are caught in a curious 'double bind' over our attitude to children. Our leaders claim to support the family. Many of them advocate a return to 'basic values'. But, of course, an equally important part of their job is to promote many of the commercial interests which threaten those values: our economic survival is tied up with their success. Looking back over the past twenty years it's hard to identify what we have achieved in practical terms to support and encourage ordinary families.

As family life is already so fragmented, the church needs to look for innovative ways of integrating adults and children – in worship and learning, but also simply in discovering new ways to have fun together. It's all too easy to slip into our society's individualistic, 'me first' mentality.

The latter half of the twentieth century has seen the family retreat into the safety and security of its own four walls at a time when our society desperately needs more of the 'community factor' – that is, men, women and children who will look out for one another and consider one another's common needs before their own. The questions we need to ask ourselves are: *Me first* or *Us first*? What double standards are we operating at home and at church? What challenges does the gospel make to our 1990s individualistic lifestyle?

A challenge to the church

The gospel calls us to an unselfish, unconditional commitment of love. It's a love that is both practical and spiritual. It has to be worked out in all our relationships, from the home outwards. As far as our children are concerned, it can't be legislated for or 'farmed out'. It can't be bought by colourful gadgetry. It is a self-giving love that accepts, welcomes, esteems, encourages, protects and upholds through various stages of growth and transition. rebellion and change. We are called to nurture a unique journey of faith into adulthood, spiritually and physically.

Children have a right to belong. The kingdom of God belongs to them and they are to be cherished, protected and nurtured in God's family in his world. They are of unique significance and are therefore to be welcomed regardless of race, religion, status, age, sex or physical disability. They are to be attended to, not by extra-curricular activities, but by the whole church family, a family which takes the rich diversity of the biblical 'household' as its inspiration. Our children belong in a web of relationships which includes young and old, single and married. These relationships will be shaped by the experience of the cross of Christ. They will be founded on costly commitment and servanthood.

The gospel view of children challenges us not only to 'think big' about children themselves. It also demands that we enlarge our thinking about what it actually means to be the church. If we agree that we should welcome children into the community of believers, then we should be asking searching questions about the kind of community we are opening up to them.

The more we can as churches encourage activities that include *all* ages, the better for our children and the better for a healthy community life, wherever we live. Where in the life of your church at present do you plan activities that mix together people of all ages and backgrounds?

Where are you now?

Some questions to explore individually or as a group:

- What do you see as the greatest benefits for children in our modern way of life?
- What do you see as its greatest dangers for children?
- What can we do in the church to support and guide our children as they face the pressures of contemporary culture?
- List four things you think our society believes about children.
- What are the major factors that have influenced these benefits?
- How are children valued today?

Recommended reading

David Porter, *Children at Play*, Kingsway, 1989

David Porter, *Children at Risk*, Kingsway, 1986

Eugene F. Provenzo Jr., *Video Kids*, Harvard University Press, 1991

Nigel Forde, 'Video Poem', *Children in the Way* video, Church of England Board of Education, 1988

Dr Griffith Thomas, *Principles of Theology*, Article 27

Robert Banks, *Going to Church in the First Century*, Hexagon Press, 1984

John Pridmore, 'All God's Children', *Third Way* magazine, 1978

For further background reference

Derek Tidball, *An Introduction to the Sociology of the New Testament*, Paternoster Press, 1983

Wayne Meeks, *The Moral World of the First Christians*, SPCK, 1987

Robert Banks, *Paul's Idea of Community*, Paternoster Press, 1980

Hans Ruedi Weber, *Jesus and the Children: Biblical resources for study and preaching*, World Council of Churches, 1979

CHAPTER THREE

MAKING CHILDREN WELCOME

Half a welcome?

It's Sunday morning. Sally and Tracey are on their way to the morning service at their local church. They attend regularly and they always arrive together. As they enter the building, members of the 'Welcome Team' greet Sally warmly by name. They do not speak to Tracey. Sally gets a handshake from one, a hug from another. Tracey gets neither.

Unfortunately the one church member who always says, 'Hello Tracey' is not there today. In her absence, Tracey's welcome follows its normal pattern – a friendly 'I can't quite remember your name' grin if she's lucky, a brief glance if she's not. In fact, today she does better than usual because, for once, instead of being expected to share with Sally, she is handed her own copy of the notice sheet.

Tracey waits quietly until Sally has finished talking and then follows her into church. During the service Sally, as she has often done before, leads the prayers. Tracey, despite her keen interest in world news and 'green' issues, has never been invited to contribute in this way …

And so it continues. Two members of the same church, two separate and distinct experiences of welcome. One is recognised, affirmed and involved; the other is often ignored, occasionally patronised and always kept firmly on the margin. Why do they continue to put up with it? Probably because, incredible as it seems, neither Sally, Tracey, nor anyone else in the church, realises that there's anything out of the ordinary in the situation. What blinds them to such blatant discrimination? The simple fact that Sally is thirty-four and Tracey, her daughter, is nine years old.

Equal value, equal welcome

If I really believe in the spiritual value and significance of children, it is going to affect how I behave towards them. For me, making children welcome, whether it's in my family life, church or recreation, is a God-given priority. Whether I am chatting to mums and their offspring in the school playground, going shopping or meeting students and their families here in Ridley College, where we now live, somehow it has become as natural as breathing for me to address the children as well as the adults.

Children are people too. I make a point of addressing and welcoming them because I firmly believe that they have a significant place and purpose in our relationships in the body of Christ.

Of course there are many in our churches already who welcome children warmly, recognise their individuality and encourage their participation. But how individuals behave towards children will have little impact on the church unless there is a wider commitment from both congregation and leadership. When marginalising children is the norm, the first step is simply to make people aware that there is a problem to be addressed. Only then can there be the will to create the sort of environment in our church life that makes welcoming children more of a possibility.

First impressions

A child's attitude to church can be affected by what happens in those first few moments after entering the building. Many children feel they are not coming voluntarily. As far as they are concerned they are there because their parents want them to be there. Their experience tells them that church is a place where adults come first. Therefore their expectation is that the adults will do their normal adult thing – talking to other adults!

The child's impression is reinforced when adults greet one another warmly, exchange news and pass on messages without even once turning to the children and welcoming or including them. Be honest, if you went somewhere several times and were never spoken to personally, or people only referred to you in a secondary sort of way, would you want to go again?

How children are welcomed at the doors of our churches is vitally important. It will set the tone of acceptance (or lack of it) throughout the rest of the service. But, as most churches will acknowledge, to be truly welcoming takes more than good intentions. You need structure and organisation: a rota, volunteers, a Welcome Desk.

Training required

Individual church members should be given the task of welcoming people as they arrive. They should be trained in simple interpersonal skills. Have you, for example, ever been greeted with a limp 'wet fish' handshake, or been embarrassed by the shyness or lack of eye-contact from the person meant to be greeting you?

Welcomers need to know how to greet people appropriately, sensitively and efficiently. (The Christian bear-hug is *not* always appropriate.) They need to know the layout of the building so that they can direct people to the toilets or crèche. They should be able to explain something about the service (for example, that it is a family service with Holy Communion), give some idea of what is likely to happen in it and indicate how long it is likely to last.

In particular, people should be trained in welcoming children.

Most children don't like being patted on the head. My younger daughter, being small, often suffers from this. She says she feels like a dog!

If it is possible, why not make a point of always including one of the children's workers in the Welcome Team? It's unrealistic to expect everyone to know the name of every child, and the children's worker is more likely to know who is who among the younger age groups. For a nine-year-old, a friendly hello is more meaningful if it comes from someone who has spent time teaching you a song, or has helped you with a craft activity and who knows a bit about your favourite computer game.

Faces send clear messages. Children are particularly skilful at picking up our unspoken, 'body language' communications. So it is important for them to see the welcomer's face clearly. If you are greeting a child, it can help if you bob down to his or her eye-level, smile and say 'Hi' and, if appropriate, take a hand or gently squeeze an arm.

A Note About Touch

Touch is a very important way for us to communicate warmth and acceptance. It should always be used sensitively and with discrimination. This is particularly the case with children. Sadly, in a society still reeling from various scandals of child abuse, this is now an area in which we need special wisdom. What is an appropriate touch from one adult, is totally inappropriate from another. Some children are more 'touch-sensitive' than others. Few parents would mind their small son or daughter receiving a motherly hug from a middle-aged matron. They may feel less comfortable with similar behaviour from that woman's adult son. What matters most, of course, is knowing the child and behaving towards him or her with sensitivity and respect.

Service Books For Children?

A very practical way to help children feel welcomed and attended to is to offer them their own book or booklet. I know of a number of churches which have their own children's song books, with clear bold type and, in some cases, illustrations as well. Have you shared a hymn book recently with a small child? It's a risky business. If he holds it with you, it's difficult to find an appropriate height; have you noticed how the words dance on a page when a little hand is holding one side? I am sure children would be encouraged to participate in worship more, if they had their own service books or sheets, in appropriate sizes for small hands and bold enough print for small children to read.

One church I know of arranged and designed their song book with children in mind, using clear colours and pictures to help children find their way around it quickly and easily. This is particularly useful if you have a worship slot in your service where most of the children's songs are sung.

Further opportunities

Working with children is a very rewarding ministry. For me the most special aspect of it has been helping to administer Communion at family services, where all God's family, in ones, twos, threes or more come to receive the symbols and signs of God's love for them. The children come too, from tiny tots to teenagers. At those moments I'm moved by what I can see in God's people; their thankfulness for his love for them and such openness and eagerness written on the children's faces.

In the Communion Service we welcome people to the Communion table and address them personally in the words of administration. But what do we do with the children? Do we welcome them and do we speak to them personally, or do they get a cursory pat on the head and a prayer spoken to mid-air?

Serving at Communion is an important privilege. It is an

opportunity to welcome and serve God's people and a time when we can in particular welcome children, encouraging them to come into God's presence and learn of his special love for them.

Towards a wider welcome

Our underlying attitudes to the value and status of our children will be reflected in the welcome we give them. If we believe children have a right to be in church and are significant *already* because of God's love for them and relationship with them, then that belief should be reflected in our attitudes, values and practical planning. If we actually believe this, then not only those who welcome at the door, but other adults and service leaders should begin to treat the children as fellow-members, rather than awkward nuisances who have to be provided for, because they happen to be there.

For many of us, children will simply start to become visible. Once that happens we have to ask ourselves searching questions about the quality of the welcome we offer them. Do we smile at them? Do we help them in the service? Do we talk to them if the opportunity arises, introduce ourselves to them and tell them a bit about ourselves? If a child *knows* who we are, he or she will be far more likely to be open with us and begin to trust us. Maybe church members regularly sit near some children or they regularly *avoid* sitting near children! If they *do* sit near children, do they know their names and the schools they go to? If they prefer to sit apart, do they know why they do?

Children sense whether they belong or not. You may dress up as clowns and shake their hands heartily, but if in your heart and spirit you would really rather they weren't there – well, you may possibly fool other adults, but you won't deceive the children.

Speak, listen and respond

How can children know that they are valued and have significance among us? The quality of our welcome and the

The Importance of the Child to God

We all need to believe in the importance of the child to God. It's no good just convincing the people responsible for welcoming. The *whole* congregation needs to be convinced. But how on earth do you do that? Here are some suggestions:

● Teaching from the pulpit.
● Teaching in small groups – home groups, if you have them.
● Pray about your own and the church's response to children.
● Make sure the children, as a group and as individuals, are on the church's prayer agenda.
● Ask the Holy Spirit to show you how the whole church can co-operate in welcoming the children and giving them a sense of belonging among you.

firmness of our belief in them as fellow-pilgrims will make a difference. And this will be demonstrated by our willingness to speak directly to our children, to listen to them and to respond to them.

Have you ever asked yourself about the times when, and the places where, you have felt significant and valued? It may be when someone has received you warmly in some way, affirmed you, or agreed with something you've said; or when someone has given you particular attention, acknowledged something you have done, or listened to you and valued what you had to say. So how in similar ways, can our children be helped to feel they are significant and valued in our services and in our worship?

One way is to speak directly to them: 'I want this morning to welcome you all to the family service and to give a special welcome to our younger brothers and sisters and to any visitors this morning.' Don't be afraid to 'direct' this greeting time: 'Will you please turn and welcome one another, and please remember to include visitors and our younger brothers and sisters in your welcome.'

Leading by example

When a ten-year-old has something to say, he wants to say it at once. 'Talk to me later', whether it comes from parent, teacher or church leader, is not a satisfactory response. Listening to children takes time and effort. If a vicar or minister stops to listen to a child and responds to what he or she has said with encouragement and affirmation, others will notice. Very soon they will catch on that children deserve the same courtesy and attentiveness that one would give to an adult.

If we stop and listen seriously to children (not half-heartedly, with one ear listening to an adult conversation), then others will notice and soon our church will become known as one which values all people – including children. Of course, we need to do more than merely respond courteously when children make their presence felt. They should be spoken to and dealt with as valued participants.

Any preacher planning a sermon or talk to a mixed-age group will have had to think out ways of holding the children's interest by making the material relevant and accessible to them. But the sermon is only a small part of the service. How are the needs of children addressed in the planning and actual structure of the worship?

I believe that children feel significant and special when they are spoken to by name, when they experience things visually and dramatically, through acting out stories and experiences. They feel they matter when they are allowed to join in, whether it's in a festal shout or a responsive reading.

I believe the gospel has power to change lives, but often I fail to allow that power to challenge and transform *my* life into the image of Christ. To be Christ-like with children, we need to receive them tenderly with open arms and open relationships – with no pretence, but with genuine affection and friendship on which trust can be built.

Start From Where You Are

How can individuals and congregations begin to take a more responsible attitude towards welcoming children? When my children were very small I always valued people who took the trouble to sit in the pew with me. I was on my own, as my husband was busy being the vicar 'up front'! As any parent knows, it can be a real struggle trying to help two (or maybe three or four) very different small children find their way through the service, helping them find their places in the book and answering endless, often necessary, questions.

I am forever grateful to the people who bothered to talk to me, help the children and show that they cared. It made a tremendous difference to me. Also, I'm certain that their friendliness made a difference to my girls.

I remember they sometimes found the readings and talks difficult to follow and understand, and I tried to explain what was happening as we went along. But while explaining to the one child, the other one still needed help and guidance too. That was when I really needed others not simply to 'baby-sit' my children, but to bring vital practical and spiritual support to them.

It is so easy to drop into the habit of not talking to others in

Where are you now?

How child-friendly is your church? Skim through this check-list to get a 'snapshot' picture of your current situation.

- Where do people sit in church?
- Is it always the same place?
- Do church members know the people sitting around them?
- Do church members know the children by name?
- How many church members pray regularly for the children?
- How many of your church members greet the children when they come into church?

church, especially children and strangers. Children need to be drawn in and won with trust: it is a very gradual process. Bothering to show straightforward practical helpfulness is a starting point that's open to all of us. As my mother would say, 'A little bit of help is worth a lot of pity.'

People are often 'held back' by the fear of intruding or being rebuffed. But we can all be encouraged to begin in small ways. Anyone can smile and say hello. It's not too difficult to talk to children about things that are relevant to them. If a child is struggling to find his way through the hymn book or service book, you might want to make a discreet offer of help. But beware of taking over and doing it all for her – that can be a real insult to a child establishing her own independence, even if it's only a matter of holding the hymn book for herself.

Maybe church members would consider allowing a small child to sit on their knee so that they can see better. Slowly, gradually, children will learn that other church members are 'OK people', who actually like them and want to talk to them, not just to Mum and Dad. It's often the very small things, gestures and words, that begin to communicate a sense of belonging – the important message that in this church it's acceptable to be a child.

- Are older members, now free of responsibility for young children, willing to sit with young families and interact with them?
- What attitude do you think church members generally have towards children being in the service? *Be honest.* Are they considered a nuisance or are they welcomed?
- What could be done in your church to make children feel more welcome?
- How can church leaders share the responsibility for our children and best support them?

Where do you want to get to?

This list provides some simple, but not too easy, challenges for any leader who has decided to adopt a more positive attitude to welcome. As a person with a leadership role within the church, I will want to:

Publicly welcome the children and help them to feel at home in the body.

Demonstrate by what I say and do that the children are welcome.

Teach and train other service and lay leaders to welcome children.

Know the children's names and to which family they belong.

Address the children specifically in the service; ask them questions; interact with them where possible.

Shake their hands as they leave or use appropriate touch.

Consider children both in the church's overall strategy, and in the planning of the church budget.

Listen to the needs of the parents and children in the church (and outside).

● Consider giving priority to encouraging recruitment, training and support of leaders for the children's and young people's work.

● Assess *how* the children's work fits into and fulfils the aims and objectives of the church.

How are you going to get there?

Maybe some people will say to themselves: 'But I am single, I'm widowed, my children have grown up. How can I participate in this responsibility?' Here are some ideas:

● Pray for the children's work leaders.

Pray for the recruitment of new leaders.

Pray for the children as they start new classes and schools at the start of each school year.

- Find out when the children's leaders meet. Pray for their planning meetings and their fellowship and witness as a leadership team.
- Pray for the children, when you know they are taking part in special events, like the Christingle service, the Family Carol service, Harvest and Mothering Sunday.

Then, although people may not necessarily feel called or equipped to be leaders in the children's work, they may go on to ask themselves if they could help in some way. Maybe they could welcome the children at the door and help them with their coats or fill in a register? Could they help with the crèche or make tea (or mix paint) at the Parents' and Toddlers' Group? There are lots of ways people can be involved, if they want to be.

To be welcomed is to be appreciated not just for who you are, but also for what you do. When the children have made an enjoyable contribution to the service, encourage people not to keep quiet about it. Instead, suggest that they send a card or letter to the leaders responsible to show appreciation and to express thanks for all their hard work. I know that many, many times I've thought to myself: 'I must write to thank and encourage Fred, or Jean, or Tony.' Sadly, I have to admit that too often my good intentions don't lead on to action. But I know that when I have taken time to write, my brief message has been greatly appreciated. Good and healthy relationships in the body of Christ can be aided and maintained if we *take time* to say (or write) 'thank you' as a *regular* discipline. Often, God has a way of nudging us and causing us to think or pray about someone or something. Encourage one another to *obey* the 'nudge' of the Spirit. Keep a little pile of thank-you cards nearby and use them regularly.

There are obviously many ways that we can be involved with children if we want to be. I just happen to believe that God doesn't let us have the luxury of time off with this issue! I believe he calls us to face right up to it, just as he did when his disciples tried to turn the children away! We must obey – not only for the sake of the future of the church, but because we are called to follow the teaching and life of Christ. It is for the sake of his kingdom that we do it.

It's very easy to ignore the obvious. In all deliberations about welcoming children into the church, we should not forget that the children themselves have opinions. All we need to do is ask them. Sadly, in church at least, the children are rarely expected to express their opinions about their needs. Away from church, however, they are frequently asked to do this. For example, as part of the National Curriculum pupils are now required to make their own reviews and assessments of how they are progressing in a particular subject; they are expected to state some agreed aims relating to their work and behaviour. Shouldn't the church also be ready to listen to the thoughts, interests and preoccupations of our children? We can learn much from their insights. We need to be asking our children, their parents and the children's workers *how* we can better accommodate their needs and share this very special *God-given* responsibility we have for them.

CHAPTER FOUR

SERVICES: WELCOME INTO WORSHIP

Once the children have got past the door, what is their experience of being in church? Do they have a sense of active involvement, or are they passive spectators? If you're not sure, sneak up to the front one Sunday and look back at the congregation. One glance at the children will tell you what's going on. Bright, focused eyes, attentive expressions, a buzz of interaction between child and adult, child and child – good news and sure signs that somebody is doing something right. It's equally easy to detect the bad news signals of listless, vacancy and 'Wish I was anywhere but here' boredom.

Let's take a look at some of the environments that children are currently experiencing in our churches.

Family services

Family services are now a well-established tradition. In general they are shorter, faster-paced and more visual than traditional services. But while their accessibility makes them the ideal opportunity for inviting 'non-church' friends and neighbours, I believe that nationally we've made slow progress with them in terms of children's basic involvement and participation.

Are children really being attended to in our family services? My observation is that often they are either patronised or ignored. In practice we have moved a long way from the idea of all-age worship. Instead we often provide services which use informality simply as a way of making church approachable for the adults in the congregation, rather than giving genuine consideration to the full age range represented in the church. And while there is nothing wrong with doing everything to make church more accessible to ordinary people, we also need to recognise that many of our so-called family services are not, in fact, serving our children.

But before we start tinkering with formats and structures, I am certain we need to take time to focus on the biblical 'big picture' of the place of children in the worshipping community of the church. If we believe children are *in* the kingdom and that worship is what God tells us to do at all times and in all places and especially *with* his people, the church, then I believe that children should be present and active in our corporate worship. They have every right to be alongside us, expressing every aspect of our lives in worship, physically, emotionally and spiritually.

At the moment, pockets of the church, from a variety of churchmanships, are actively recognising children as fellow-pilgrims. They are ordering their worship and liturgy in a way that includes them and nurtures them. But they are still in a minority.

From various responses I have received from children's workers and diocesan advisers, the overall situation seems to be that most parishes hold a monthly family service. Although these can take a variety of forms, I believe most of them belong in one of two main categories: (1) all-age worship and (2) the 'split' family service.

All-age worship

All-age worship offers a genuine place of participation where all age groups can be together in worship, prayer, fellowship and learning. Here, more than anywhere else, the welcome given should be the same for all members of the congregation, regardless of age.

In many ways I see all-age worship as the ideal. It follows closely the Old Testament pattern of the child being in the midst of the worshipping community. It reflects the 'cross-generational' involvement of the early church.

From my experience of planning such services in St Michael-le-Belfrey in York, I would say that introducing all-age worship, requires a high degree of commitment from the church leadership, children's and young people's workers, and music and worship leaders. In order for all-age worship to function well, *all ages* need to be involved in the planning, or at least representatives of all age groups. Our group in York met weekly to plan and pray together. Success depends upon a high degree of team commitment, good communication, efficient administration and, of course, inspiration!

Children are children!

All-age worship is not about finding lowest common denominators. Adults are not children. Children are not adults. It's important to recognise the difference.

Penny Frank is Director of the Church Pastoral Aid Society's Youth and Children Division. I agree with her when she suggests that one of the reasons for the relatively slow development of all-age worship is our habit of trying to make children behave like adults. Children learn much about their faith simply by 'being around' adults who are worshipping – but that on its own won't do!

We both believe that God wants children to *be* children and that God delights in children *as* children. Jesus treated children as children and received and welcomed them as such. It troubles me deeply that as a church we are following the culture of the day, encouraging children to become young adults in fashion, musical tastes and attitudes, not allowing them to develop emotionally, mentally, physically and spiritually with due regard for their age and stage of faith.

The introductory sentence in the service of baptism of children in the Anglican Alternative Service Book says 'Children who are too young to profess the Christian faith are baptised on the understanding that they are brought up as Christians in the family of the Church.' Do we *really* mean that? It sometimes feels as if the church spends a lot of its time trying to keep the children out, not bringing them up 'within'. I sometimes wonder why we bother to baptise our children only to 'excommunicate' them immediately afterwards!

More than lip service

Penny Frank raises an interesting point about our underlying attitudes and openness to children. She believes that, at the moment, most adults are happy to subscribe to the belief that our children are part of the church of today and not, as many used to think of them, merely the church of tomorrow in waiting.

They use the fashionable, 'theologically correct' language because they want to be heard to say the right things. But do they really mean what they say? Penny is concerned that in many cases the development of family services during the last two decades has been driven by motives that have little do with children.

The family service solved a problem for many church leaders who were finding it difficult to recruit regular committed leaders for their children's work. Members didn't want to miss out on the service in order to be with the children! Many churches solved the problem by keeping the children in with them. But it wasn't really all-age anything! It was merely a conventional service with something slotted-in for the children without necessarily altering any of the rest of the service structure. The justification for this was that it would help children get used to what church was really like and that it would prepare them for eventual adult membership. This, of course, assumes that they will still be in church by that time, which is most unlikely given the present statistics. According to the 1989 English Church Census only ten per cent of adults and fourteen per cent of children under the age of fifteen presently attend church.

The 'split' family service

The split family service is where children of all ages remain in the service, usually for the first half-hour or so, after which they leave to meet elsewhere in their various age groups. Some churches follow the same teaching themes across all the age groups, including the sermon series. Others follow a co-ordinated programme for some of the age groups with, say, the five- to eleven-year-olds following a separate theme from the older children and teenagers.

The split family service is the one most likely to fall between two stools and sit on neither. Sometimes the adults can become frustrated because they are impatient to get on with what they feel is 'their bit' of the service. By the same token the children are often not clear why they are obliged to sit through the adult part of the service. Often they can't wait to get out to their specially planned activities where they are personally welcomed and made to feel significant.

In the children's group they do things appropriate for their age group, often of a participative, 'hands-on' nature. They have fun and sing songs they understand and enjoy. I think I can understand why, on the whole, children prefer to be in the children's group rather than in church!

It is important to add that the 'split' family service continues to offer an opportunity for teaching activities appropriate to different age groups. Adults do not learn in the same way as children do, and vice versa. What is vital is that the part of the service which is shared, is truly shared, so that all sense that they are worshipping together.

Encouraging participation

How can we ensure that children are participants rather than spectators in our services? The first question we need to ask is, 'Do we really *want* them to participate?' If not, why not? Is the task simply too difficult? Or might the results be too noisy? Or is the whole area of children's involvement simply not our cup of tea?

If any of those responses ring true, then we have to face the tough question, 'Just who is church for?' Does it exist simply to attend to us as individuals, to service and encourage us on our personal walk of faith? Or is its task bigger than that – to witness to the world an alternative model of community and to welcome and disciple young and old in their *shared* journey of faith?

God meets us all as individuals, and deals with us as such. But Christianity is not an individualistic religion. Basically I'm not in church for me. I'm in church because God tells me to be with my sisters and brothers in worship and fellowship, to break bread together with them, serve the poor and minister to one another's needs spiritually and practically.

The truth is that I am primarily in church for God first, for my sisters and brothers (of all ages) second, and finally for myself.

Opening doors

Sadly, some churches remain closed to the idea that children should be present with adults in at least some of the services. Although regrettable, it's a fact that has to be acknowledged. It should make us all the more willing to work at educating and motivating ministers, church councils and congregations to discover new ways of making Sunday worship accessible, enjoyable and worshipful for our younger brothers and sisters.

One diocesan children's adviser I heard from is convinced that parishes are slowly improving in the way they deal with children. Another said that most churches in her diocese try to involve children, without trying to make the service seem totally child-

---

Check On Resources

Some dioceses have well-developed training and support for clergy and children's workers, including training on all-age worship, how to hold family services and co-ordinate programme-planning across the age groups. Anyone with responsibility for the development of work with children should know the answers to the following questions:

- Who is the children's adviser in your area?
- What training, support or resources are available for planning and organising family services or all-age worship events?
- What other organisations are there in your area (or nationally) which may be able to provide training, support and help for developing a 'whole church' strategy for the development of work with children? (Good starting points: the Church Pastoral Aid Society, Scripture Union.)

---

centred. She also commented on an interesting mismatch between the way leaders and children's workers view the welcome given to children. While most church leaders would say that children are made welcome in their churches, many of the people who work week by week with those children would disagree.

Focus on Worship

What is worship? I believe our chief purpose as Christians is to worship God. But what does that mean? How do we do it?

Andrew Maries, formerly our Worship Director in York, has now set up the Keynote Trust, which encourages church musicians in their spiritual vision and commitment to their congregations. Andrew says that worship involves the *whole* of life – spiritual, emotional, physical, intellectual, at home, at work, in the community. Worship is the expression of that life in a variety of situations.

Andrew also describes worship as a 'summary' of our lives – individually and corporately – as the people of God. He goes on to point out a number of elements that need to be present, in order for God's people to worship:

Worship should reflect where we are with God.

Worship should be a place of freedom, a place where you can be real about yourself.

Worship should be where you offer yourself, your own unique gifts and responses into the whole life of God's people.

Worship should have a 'family' feel about it. As we worship there should be a sense of informality, spontaneity, enjoyment and celebration. But worship should also have a sensitivity to sadness and hurt, a 'weeping with those who weep'.

Worship should be real, not false or empty praise, or crying 'peace' where there is no peace.

Worship should be many-faceted, reflecting many different personalities, experiences, backgrounds, tastes.

Worship should be a place of reconciliation and should lead us towards becoming one whole people; it should lead us into accepting, loving and honouring each other, respecting different gifts and approaches.

Worship should be a place to change and grow; it should be a 'dialogue' place, where we are in conversation with God and where he speaks and ministers to us; it should be a place where we acknowledge our lack of wholeness and where we begin to face ourselves in God's light.

Worship should be a place where spiritual gifts are exercised and where we are open to challenge.

Worship should be a place of faith, expectancy and hope, in which we believe that God can and will do something. Corporate worship can 'lift' individuals and renew their faith and hope when they feel weak by themselves.

(Adapted from a paper by Andrew Maries, 'An evaluation of worship at St Michael-le-Belfrey', December 1993.)

The art of worship is to enable people to open up to God and to each other so that we can realise our corporate identity as the body of Christ and operate as such.

There are, of course, many elements that we use to serve and

Qualities for Leading Worship

The worship leaders should be more than musicians and singers. The following list highlights nine qualities which I believe are the key to good worship leading. Worship leaders ideally should:

- Be at the heart of the life of the church, committed to it and supportive of its leadership.
- Be trained in worship leading ('on the job' training counts).
- Have servant hearts and an openness to God's Holy Spirit, so that they can encourage, serve, enable and inspire others.
- Be able to play music and lead in a way that encourages others and catches them up in worship. (Music groups can often end up playing *to* the congregation rather than drawing, 'capturing' and encouraging it into worship.)
- Be able in an all-age worship context to keep abreast of popular children's music and worship and be bold in leading actions and movements to songs as appropriate.
- Be in touch with what's happening spiritually in the church among God's people.
- Take seriously the holiness of their own lives. They need to be examples of worship as well as leading others into worship.
- Be open to God's Spirit to speak to them, prompt them and touch them.
- Be able to integrate the practical and spiritual, the sacred and the secular.

enhance worship. Among them are music, liturgy, movement, dance, banners, candles, flowers. All of these will reflect both the unity of the congregation and its rich diversity of gifts, abilities and personalities.

All ages together

Worship in an all-age setting needs to be carefully planned. Its success depends on a background of regular prayer, sharing among the leaders of the church, and regular contact and liaison between them and the children's and youth workers. It's vital that leaders are in touch with the interests and tastes of *all* ages. If the 'cringe factor' is to be avoided, it is particularly important to have a feel for the loves, hates and preoccupations of today's children and young people. Do you, for example, know what song is currently 'flavour of the month' with each age group from late teens downwards? Do you happen to know if the children actually like the songs you sing in church? Has anyone tried asking them? Have the children ever been invited to join the worship group and help lead the actions in the children's songs? Have children ever been included in the worship group? Some children are very accomplished musicians, some have beautiful voices and most have lots of enthusiasm. At one stage we ran a children's band, which was very popular, but required a very high degree of commitment and hard work from the leaders.

Children have been known to lead the main worship slot in churches, playing their own instruments. I had some seven- to ten-year-olds in our children's work who did this very competently, with help from a leader. They played drums, recorders, tambourines and trumpets and, more than once, taught the whole congregation songs they had composed.

Children can be wonderfully enthusiastic in worship, but we have to catch their interest and take them with us into God's presence. All-age services can be noisy and appear messy and disjointed. But if the worship is of a good quality, it will draw the body, old and young together, in harmony. It will bring peace in the middle of noise. It will build expectation and faith and help us all, children and adults together, to be more aware of God's presence and of what he is saying to us individually and corporately.

Look out!

Children experience the world through their senses, drinking in experiences in great gulps through their eyes and ears. They are visual before they are verbal. They imbibe words only in small sips. So why, when they come to church, do we expect them to swallow words (most of them difficult and unfamiliar) by the gallon?

Children respond spontaneously to a lively, colourful environment. Most primary school classrooms are crammed with colourful displays, vibrant artwork and interesting objects. In contrast, church must seem monochrome and wordy to our children. So what about including *more* that is visual and colourful in our church life?

Banners. Bold, colourful fabric hangings can transform a dull interior and bring warmth. They are an aid to worship and prayer. They can help focus and sustain our worship. Children can make banners, designing them as well as sewing or sticking them together. Our children made banners for a Christingle service which had the theme of 'Jesus the light'. They were amazingly creative with their ideas and they produced a wonderful set of six banners which, when displayed, were greatly appreciated by the whole church.

Flowers. I love flowers, so maybe that's why I notice them particularly. But I also notice that if there has been a wedding at church, the children are drawn to the flower arrangements with their beautiful colours and shapes, the ribbons and scent. Flowers too can be an aid to worship and a colourful expression of the variety of colour and beauty in God's kingdom. Why not set aside one Sunday when the children are allowed to fill the church with their own special flower arrangements?

Visual aids. How much use does your church make of visual aids, drama or participation in order to help sustain the interest of children and young people? The overhead projector can be used in a variety of ways: to illustrate a talk, to allow people to focus on and respond to something God has been saying or doing, or to help create an atmosphere of faith.

Now that you can photocopy onto acetate (using special acetate film), there is a wider range of possibilities for a more creative use of the overhead projector. In the prayer time you could put up pictures of the part of the world you are praying for. There could be appropriate pictures when you are praying for the sick or the bereaved. This would particularly help young children focus their attention and their prayers. We had one very gifted artist in our congregation who made a set of cut-out silhouettes of the stations of the cross. When projected in a darkened church, these were incredibly striking and awe-inspiring. Many people in that Good Friday service were drawn into a very special time of intimate worship with God because of those silhouettes.

This is just one of the techniques that can be used to focus the attention of the whole congregation, helping us all enter into worship with a little more understanding and confidence. The overhead projector, of course, is not the only form of visual aid, nor should it be. Flannelgraphs, cartoons, whiteboards and puppets can all capture people's attention. Drama, mime and dance or any *involving* activity helps sustain the interest of both adults and children.

Responsibility

It is our own responsibility to prepare ourselves and our children for worship. But we cannot escape the fact that we are affected by our surroundings. There's no such thing as a neutral

---

About crèches

The Sunday morning crèche is a much-appreciated facility offered by many churches. Mum and dad can leave their baby or toddler in capable hands and are then free to take part in the service unencumbered by their offspring.

But I have to admit that, as much as possible. I would encourage parents to persevere with their children – particularly in family services, ideally in regular services as well – rather than 'parking them' in the crèche. If children are bored with the service and parents are struggling with bad behaviour, that is another matter altogether and needs talking out sensitively with the parents, offering them support and practical advice about how to help a child engage in the service. I am concerned about the messages we are sending our children when we put them regularly in the crèche, rather than taking them with us to the service.

On the whole, I'm in favour of 'emergency only' crèches, to which a parent may take a tired, tearful child during the service. If the child is unhappy or upset, he needs mum or dad with him until he is ready to go back to the service.

---

environment. Either it is an obstacle to our growing in faith and giving ourselves in worship, or it becomes an aid and encouragement which causes us – adults and children together – to draw closer to one another in fellowship and closer to God.

Although we bear our own responsibility for preparation for worship, we come as the body of Christ into our services and, as the body of Christ, we enter into a shared responsibility for the nurture, well-being and wholeness of everybody in God's family – and that includes children!

My prayer is that we will all be given a new vision, or renewed in our existing vision, for a church that genuinely shares responsibility for our younger brothers and sisters, both practically and spiritually.

Where are you now?

Check-out 1: accessibility

How accessible are our church meetings and services? Is the way they are planned and organised appropriate to the needs and interests of all, or only some, of the congregation?

What is worship and how can we make it attractive, participative and meaningful for children?

How appropriate is the liturgy we use?

How appropriate is our physical 'worship environment'?

Check-out 2: involvement

How many of the following 'involvement strategies' are you using at the moment?

● Children's band or choir

Children helping to lead worship

Children reading the lessons

Children writing or involved with a dramatic reading

Drama; mime; dance; banners

Taking the collection

Interaction in the sermon with questions and answers

Liturgical responses with children in mind

Children writing and reading their own prayers

Check-out 3: participation

Answering the following questions will give an idea of current commitment to the idea of 'Everybody Welcome':

Are children spoken to as valued participants by the service leaders?

Can children follow the service easily in an appropriate book, on a service sheet or on the overhead projector screen?

Is the printing you use clear and easy to follow for small children?

- Are your service and hymn books of the size a child can hold comfortably?
- Can the children see the service leader? Do they all have a good view of what is happening at the front?

A place that allows and enables a child to participate, which is welcoming and which makes the child feel valued and special – that's the sort of place that a child *will want to visit again*. We need to ask ourselves if our churches are such places? Are they *accessible, understandable and relevant* to our smaller brothers and sisters as well as to adults?

Where do you want to get to?

Realism and resources

Open access? Worship which is attractive, participative, meaningful – but why, in the first place, *should* our services appeal to children? Because, as I have argued in Chapter 2, I believe the Bible teaches us so. Through the Old Testament pattern of life and worship and through Jesus' teaching and engagement with children, it is clear that children belong at the heart of the life and worship of God's people.

Many of us may subscribe to the belief that children are a vital part of the life of the church. But in practice we organise very little that is accessible and understandable, challenging and fun for them. Sunday school may well be the only place where children have any kind of positive experience. How can we extend this to the mainstream, public life of God's people of all ages?

Where? All of us have to work within certain structural 'givens' – unavoidable limitations imposed by architecture and tradition. There's no such thing as a perfect situation! Listed buildings, inflexible seating arrangements, church councils, financial limitations – all of these will mould the way we do things. Some churches may have to work within a set framework of liturgy or an established pattern of services; others may have to adapt to a variety of groups of very different ages with very different expectations of worship.

But these structural 'facts of life' should not prevent us from making an honest assessment of the accessibility of our worship. I believe that there's a particular need to look at the services at which young children (from zero to twelve years of age) are likely to be present – and that includes everything from regular family services, the church festivals (Easter, Pentecost and Christmas) and the other times of special focus (Harvest, Missionary Sunday, Covenant Sunday, Education Sunday etc). On any or all of these occasions, do we plan the services in such a way that the different elements of worship, prayer, teaching and ministry are not only accessible and interesting to children, but also actively inclusive of them as well?

How do we create the right setting? How does church feel to a child? I have often wondered if it must sometimes seem rather like school, but with all the exciting bits left out. Today's 'hands-on' style of education aims to engage the child's interest with a variety of absorbing 'learning experiences': computers, videos, technology, drama and investigation are now familiar aspects of classroom life.

Of course, the primary function of the church isn't to be school (even if it feels like it sometimes), but to worship God. However, whether we like it or not, when it comes to catching and keeping the interest of children, the church *is* in competition with school, and also with sport, entertainment and leisure activities – in fact every aspect of life which has a claim on our children's interest and allegiance. It's a challenge we ignore at our peril.

Finding the right people. If you have children yourself, or work with them, you will know from experience when you have captured their interest and when you have lost them. Some people are gifted story-tellers and have children hanging on every word. Some speakers and leaders are lively, charismatic, colourful figures who demand attention. Clearly, we are not all gifted in these ways. But often, within our congregations, there are many undiscovered people who have special gifts as communicators with both adults and children. If that is the case:

● How are they identified, encouraged and trained in the life of the church?
● How are their gifts used?

If you have any such gifted communicators, do try to use them. The task of preparation for speaking and leadership is less onerous for them than it is for someone who doesn't have a natural feel or calling for work with children. As a bonus, of course, they release the minister to have a more overall role of leadership.

Looking at liturgy

How appropriate is the liturgy we use? Before we can answer that question we also need to ask, 'In what setting or "cultural context" are we planning to use the liturgy and how effectively will it communicate there?' Readings, responses and ritual that may be entirely appropriate in one situation may well prove, in different circumstances, to be disastrously inappropriate. In other words, before we can explore the 'What?' of liturgy, we need to answer questions of 'Where?', 'When?' and 'How?'

Since the earliest formation of household gatherings, Christians have debated the issue of cultural relevance. Over the years, the guardians of our faith have been concerned to maintain certain boundaries and to ensure that local congregations at worship have had a sense of belonging to the wider church. Therefore, as a general rule, the church has been cautious in its approach to changes in either the ingredients or the structure of its services.

Although many of us may long for more flexibility and adaptability within our liturgical framework, there are many ways in which we can help people (including children) to understand and find meaning in it. For example:

81

- Do adults and children understand the liturgy?
- Who explains to children and adults in your congregation the meaning of the liturgy you use?
- Do church members, young and old, understand the significance of the Confession and Absolution?
- Do they appreciate the response they call for?
- Similarly, do church members understand why we say the Prayer of Humble Access and the Prayer of Thanksgiving in the Communion Service?
- Do children as well as adults understand why the Creed and the Commandments are regularly used?

Prayers. I have noticed that prayers are often led by a couple, sometimes by a family, occasionally by a group of singles. In terms of modelling God's family, it would be good if the 'prayer slot' was sometimes led by adults (single as well as married) *and* children. Children are quite capable of writing and reading their own prayers, albeit with a little oversight from a friendly adult. Children may not always want to read their prayers from 'up front', but they may give Mum, Dad or the children's worker permission to read them out for them. It may be helpful for them to write their prayers on an overhead projector acetate.

Responsive prayers. These can work well when all ages are present in a service. The *Dramatised Bible* is an excellent source of responsive prayers. At the end of this chapter are some examples of responsive readings, a confession, a statement of faith and prayers, adapted from the *Dramatised Bible*. In my experience it is much more involving for children when the more wordy parts of the service are broken up by the use of lively responsive readings and prayers.

Service cards. Where possible, use a service card or sheet that is appropriate for children as well as adults. Use bold type and adequate spacing of lines. Crowded small letters are very difficult for a small child to decipher. If a particular form of service is used regularly, a laminated, child-proof card is

Giving Talks in an All-Age Context

I have already mentioned that the *Dramatised Bible* is a good resource for readings and prayers. But what about the actual 'talk-slot', probably the hardest element of the service to get right? Whoever you aim at, somebody feels excluded! There are a few key points to remember:

● Keep it simple in structure – don't be too broad-ranging.
● Use simple sentence construction.
● Use simple words. Avoid 'ecclesiological', 'contextualisation' and 'eschatological' – believe it or not, I've heard all these in family service talks!
● Talk *to* the congregation, not *at* them.
● Grab everyone's attention at the start – tell a joke, use a visual aid.
● Get everyone focused on the theme or subject.
● Ask questions and encourage interaction.
● Avoid the pulpit. As long as you are visible, it's better to stay close to your audience.
● Encourage the children to come nearer, preferably with an adult, so that they can hear and see better.
● Use a variety of visual aids. There's more to life than an overhead projector!
● Be enthusiastic – avoid a monotonous, parsonical voice!
● Aim for an ideal length of ten to twelve minutes in order to hold all age groups.

Big agenda

The pulpit is not the only place where teaching happens. People learn by watching, copying, participating, doing, answering questions, being caught up in the atmosphere of faith, listening, praying, pondering, meditating, joining in with liturgy and even conversations after the service. We often fall into the trap of trying to cover everything in the sermon or talk. The whole service should communicate the theme.

preferable to paper. For one-off events, consider printing a folded sheet of paper with all the songs on, so that children (and adults) are spared a paper-chase through three or four different books. A service card or sheet could include:

- The regular liturgy and the directions needed for the smooth running of the service.
- Clear directions for when something is said all together.
- Relevant notices: announcements of births, engagements, marriages and other church family news.
- News about missionary and other prayer needs, maybe including a local school as part of a prayer rota for your area.

Those of us involved in the planning and leading of all-age services desperately need more creative materials and resources, in order to make our liturgy relevant and understandable for children and adults.

It was interesting to discover in York that our family service was the place where some new Christians found it easier to have an initial sense of belonging. They could more easily follow the structure and feel included.

Our liturgy and structures must not be so inflexible that they do not allow for the germination of new ideas and approaches. Nor must they be so fluid that there is no discernible pattern. Abandoning structures altogether would be to risk throwing out the baby with the bath water. I have a strong commitment to the historical foundations of my church. I also know from my teaching experience that children need pattern and structure in order to have a secure base from which to explore and learn. In terms of all ages worshipping together, the most accessible and helpful liturgy is one that has form and pattern but which is involving, focused and flexible.

Make the most of your environment

The spiritual nurture of our children is the prime responsibility of the parents. But it is also a shared responsibility with the whole church. This has far-reaching implications, not just for how we welcome and receive children, but also for how our services are planned and ordered to include them as participants rather than spectators.

How we think affects what we do. If we are serious about integrating our 'theology of the child' into the values, structures and patterns of our church, then we may have to consider making changes to our buildings, furniture and equipment.

Buildings. In every situation there are unalterable facts which simply have to be lived with, or worked around. Many churches meet in old, beautiful (but poorly lit and draughty) historic buildings, often with little or no cloakroom facilities. How can we work more creatively with our 'givens' to produce a more accessible and welcoming warm interior to our church building, hall or meeting-place?

Lighting. Getting this right can make a huge difference. Gloomy interiors always affect children. Also, for relatively modest expense it is possible to install a dimmer system, making it possible to alter light levels. This can be a great help when using the overhead projector.

Heating. This must be the bane of many a church council or minister! Heating systems, particularly in old buildings, are often both costly and inefficient. Obviously a warm building has great advantages in terms of creating a welcoming and comfortable atmosphere. Concerning children, check the following:

● Are the heating arrangements adequate in the crèche?
● Have the appliances (like gas fires) been checked recently?
● Are there adequate guards around heaters and fires in rooms used by children?

Furniture. More and more churches are reordering their interiors to adapt them to their present needs. Many now have flexible seating arrangements (no more fixed pews!) with chairs that can be linked together but also used separately. Many churches are now carpeted, creating all sorts of benefits for both children and the elderly. Carpet creates a more homely atmosphere, is good to sit and play on, deadens noise and is great to dance on!

Children's furniture. How important is child-size furniture? We don't want either the church or the children's work to feel like school, but on the other hand, if we don't have child-size tables and chairs, we are very limited in what can be done with the children. I have been in churches where there are a few rows of small chairs at the front of church for children to sit on. This works best in a small church building where Mum, Dad or another friendly adult can keep an eye on them. If the area at the front of church is carpeted, parents can come and sit with their children as appropriate. Quite a few churches invite the children to come forward to the front of church if there is a baptism, which is a lovely way of including the children in the welcoming of a new member.

What about the appropriateness of the furniture in the crèche? Crèche facilities are often limited, but ideally should consist of a box of toys, a comfortable, safe, warm floor, adequate heating and ventilation, a changing mat, potty, spare pants, disposable nappies, baby cream, a few spare clothes and an accessible first aid kit. In York, we found a couple of chairs of the appropriate height and shape (high back, no arms) in which mothers could nurse or feed their babies. Again, it helps people feel they are considered and wanted.

Quite a few churches I know have created an area at the back of the church that can be closed off and used as a crèche, for other meetings and for coffee after church. This area can also be used as an extension to the main body of the church, creating extra seating when needed.

Most small children end up sitting on knees or standing on pews, so that they can see what's happening. If children can't see the leader or speaker, they quickly lose interest. This means that while parents have a responsibility to find the most appropriate places for their children to sit, churches need to look at how their buildings can be made more accessible and comfortable for children.

Coping with change

Change doesn't come quickly, easily or without cost. We have to be determined and organised enough to do something about it. Sometimes it's simply a matter of sowing seeds. The last thing an overworked minister needs is more people beating him or her over the head with criticisms about things not being good enough. Find out the realistic cost of change, taking into account what you will do about services while the change is taking place. Weigh the advantages against the disadvantages and above all 'think growth' – especially in this Decade of Evangelism.

Resources

Mothering Sunday family service

Sunday 10 March 1991, Saint Michael-le-Belfrey, York.

Leader: Jesus said, we are to love him even more than we love our mother: 'Anyone who loves his mother more than me is not worthy of me.'

All: Lord, help us to love our mothers and to love you as you deserve.

Leader: Jesus said, we can be like a mother to him: 'Whoever does God's will is my brother and sister and mother.'

All: Lord, we often do what our mothers want; help us always to do what you want.

Leader: Jesus said we must be like a mother to one another: 'No-one who has left home or brothers or sisters, or mother or father or children for me and the gospel will fail to receive a hundred times as much in this present age: homes, brothers, sisters, mothers, children...'

All: Lord, help us to open our homes and be family to all who love you.

Leader: Jesus said that he will honour the unnoticed ones: those who have made themselves last, to serve their families, or to serve his people: 'Many who are first will be last and the last first.'

All: Lord, help us to serve one another, but to treat no one as our servant, and help us to honour those whom you honour. Amen.

[★]

Leader: The church is wherever God's people are praising, singing their thanks for joy on this day. We give you praise

All: For a mother's heart in the heart of God.

Leader: The church is wherever disciples of Jesus remember his story and walk in his way. We give you praise

All: For a mother's heart in the heart of God.

Leader: The church is wherever God's people are helping, caring for neighbours in sickness and in need. We give you praise

All: For a mother's heart in the heart of God.

Leader: The church is wherever God's people are sharing the words of the Bible in gift and in deed. We give you praise

All: For a mother's heart in the heart of God.

Preparing the Way

The following example was taken from the *Dramatised Bible* (Bible Society) and was used in a series of two family services planned around the life of John the Baptist.

Week 1

Leader: The Angel said: 'Don't be afraid Zechariah! God has heard your prayer and your wife Elizabeth will bear you a son. You are to name him John.'

All: *'How glad and happy you will be and how happy many others will be when he is born! He will be a great man in the Lord's sight.'*

Leader: 'He must not drink any wine or strong drink. From his birth he will be filled with the Holy Spirit and he will bring back many of the people of Israel to the Lord their God.'

All: *'He will go ahead of the Lord, strong and mighty like the prophet Elijah. He will bring fathers and children together again; he will turn disobedient people back to the way of the righteous; he will get the Lord's people ready for him.'*

Leader: This is the word of the Lord.

All: *Thanks be to God.*

Week 2

Leader: The word of the Lord came to John, the son of Zechariah, in the desert. He went throughout the whole territory of the River Jordan, preaching:

All: *'Turn away from your sins and be baptised and God will forgive your sins.'*

Leader: As it is written in the prophet Isaiah:

All: *Someone is shouting in the desert, 'Get the road ready for the Lord; make a straight path for him to travel. Every valley must be filled up, every hill and mountain levelled off. The winding roads must be made straight and the rough paths made smooth. All mankind will see God's salvation.'*

Leader: Crowds of people came out to John to be baptised by him. He said to all of them:

All: *'I baptise you with water, but someone is coming who is* *much greater than I am. I am not good enough even to untie his sandals. He will baptise you with the Holy Spirit and fire.'*

Confession

Leader: Let us admit to God the sin which always confronts us.

All: *Lord God, we have done evil in your sight; we have sinned against you alone. We are sorry and repent. Have mercy upon us according to your love. Wash away our wrongdoing and cleanse us from our sin. Renew a right spirit within us and restore us to the joy of your salvation, through Jesus Christ our Lord. Amen.*

Leader: May the God of forgiveness show us his mercy, forgive us our sins and bring us to everlasting life, through Jesus Christ our Lord. Amen.

Statement of Faith

Leader: We say together in faith:

All: *Holy, Holy, Holy is the Lord God Almighty, who was and is and is to come.*

Leader: We believe in God the Father, who created all things.

All: *For by his will they were created and have their being.*

Leader: We believe in God the Son, who was slain.

All: *For with his blood, he purchased us for God, from every tribe and language, from every people and nation.*

Leader: We believe in God the Holy Spirit.

All: *The Spirit and the Bride say 'Come!' Even so, come, Lord Jesus. Amen.*

CHAPTER FIVE

CHILDREN AND HOLY COMMUNION

If he pushed forward with his toes and used the rail to pull himself up, Henry discovered that he could see the lady at the other end with the funny green hat. Mr Froggatt had just taken the big cup back from her and wiped it with his hanky. 'Mrs Froggatt will be cross,' he thought. Henry's mum would be if he went around wiping cups and things with his hanky.

The vicar was handing out the bits of bread and was now half way along the row. The hat lady got up and a man knelt down in her place. He had almost no hair at all. Henry always saw him at church, and he always looked unhappy. Perhaps it was because of not having any hair. Perhaps if someone smiled at him it would make him happier. Henry pulled himself up as far as he could and managed to smile for half a second before a firm hand brought him back to earth. He added smiling to his mental list. Running, picking your nose, peeling chewing gum off your knees and now smiling. You just have to kneel there and do nothing at all. 'Nothing, nothing, nothing,' he hummed. 'Henry, stop it!' He added humming to the list.

At least there was the shaking hands bit. That was good. He was good at shaking hands. And people were allowed to smile then. But not when they were kneeling down. The peas of the Lord. Does Jesus have peas for Sunday dinner too? The vicar was giving Yvonne her bit of bread now. A very little bit. And next it was Henry's mum. And her bit of bread. And after a forever of doing nothing, at last the vicar put his big hand on Henry's head

91

and said a prayer and Henry said 'Amen!' and frowned hard to make sure the vicar did not catch him smiling.

When they got home Henry cut up some bread very carefully, which is a tricky thing to do with invisible bread. And an invisible knife can easily cut you because you can't see it at all. Making himself as big as possible and putting on a face as close to the vicar's as he could manage, Henry shuffled around handing out the pieces of bread to everyone in the house. He walked very solemnly up to Auntie Angela. She smiled. 'You're not allowed to smile.' 'Oh dear! Why not?' 'Because Jesus doesn't want you to.' 'Oh, yes he does.' 'Not when you have your bread, he doesn't.' Henry changed to being as thin as possible with a Mr Froggatt face and held out the margarine tub. She sipped. 'Mmm, delicious!' 'You've got to say Amen.' 'Mmm delicious, Amen!' she said and drained the whole tubful.

Henry found Jerry Bowum the rabbit lying behind the beanbag. Jerry Bowum was not very good at kneeling. 'Is he going to get some bread as well?' smiled Auntie Angela. 'No,' said Henry in a tone of voice which shows that it is absolutely obvious that no sensible vicar would ever give a piece of bread to a small blue rabbit. 'He can have a prayer.'

(*Henry and the Rabbit,* David Bell, CPAS, 1990)

The heart of the matter

The Lord's Supper, the Eucharist, the breaking of bread, Holy Communion – whatever name it is give, the commemoration in bread and wine of Christ's death is central to the Christian experience of worship.

The extraordinary 'ordinariness' of the simple act of sharing bread and wine takes us to the heart of what God has done for us through Jesus. Communion focuses our attention on grace. And as God's free gift of salvation is available to all, what could be more natural than to include our children when, as a church family, we gather at the Communion table.

But while Communion speaks eloquently of grace, it also calls for a conscious, deliberate response to that grace. Surely such a response involves a degree of mature reflection? How can a young child respond in a sufficiently adult way? Many would conclude that the innate seriousness of Communion demands that children wait until they are old enough to make a thoughtful, self-aware reply to God's invitation.

In recent years there has been a considerable ground swell of opinion among parents, children's work leaders and clergy about the whole issue of admitting children to Communion. Should they have to wait until they have been confirmed? Or should they be allowed to receive the bread and wine alongside their parents?

This is how children are welcomed into the church at Baptism:

> We welcome you into the Lord's family. We are members together of the body of Christ; we are children of the same heavenly Father; we are inheritors together of the kingdom of God. We welcome you.
>
> (*The Alternative Service Book,* 1980, p.248)

That's some welcome! But do we really mean it? I find it difficult to make sense of the validity of those words, when in practical day-to-day terms our children are only grudgingly welcomed, nurtured or encouraged in their own journeys of faith. And, of course, it is hardly surprising that the children and parents of an emancipated generation in the church find it hard to make sense of the exclusion of children at the Communion rail.

Current concerns

The service of Holy Communion is central to Christian life and worship. In recent years there has been a move towards a more regular weekly pattern of celebration. At the same time, there has been an increasing emphasis on participation in worship and the development of a widespread pattern of regular family services in many churches. It is not surprising that the question of children's participation has been highlighted.

Since the 1970s there has also been considerable theological debate not only about children and Communion, but also about the meaning of Communion itself, which has led many churches to examine what they are doing and why they are doing it.

We have also experienced a renewed understanding of the church as the people of God, coupled with a belief that the church needs to be a 'sign' and a model to those outside it. One of the main impacts of this renewal movement, particularly on Evangelicals, has been a refocusing on the importance of Holy Communion.

The Wider Context

World-wide cultural changes have implications on the question of children's participation in the church. The following was written for the thirtieth anniversary of the Universal Declaration of the Rights of the Child.

Here are the rights of children: Whoever we are, wherever we live. Protect us. Allow us to grow, in freedom and with dignity.

Everyone of us shall have a name and a land to call our own.

Keep us warm and shelter us. And if we are sick, nurse and comfort us.

If we are handicapped, either in body or mind, treasure us especially and give us the care we need to live happily in the world.

Keep our families together and if we have no family look after us and love us, just the same.

Teach us well, so we may enjoy the gifts of the world. But let us play, too, for some things we must discover for ourselves.

In times of trouble, help us first, for we are the future of the world.

Spare us from those who would be cruel and use us badly.

Leave us free to follow our religion in peace and without criticism.

Let us be proud of the colour of our skins. Have pride in us.

Whoever we are, wherever we live, let all these things be the inheritance of every child.

(*For Every Child*, published in association with UNICEF, 1989)

Increasing ecumenical discussions and consultations have made churches more aware of one another's practices. This has brought about an increasing openness to learn from one another's liturgical traditions. For example, Protestant churches are more aware of what happens in the Orthodox Church, where infants receive Communion from the day they are baptised. Similarly, Protestant churches are increasingly aware that Roman Catholics admit young children to Communion.

Inevitably, there has also been increasing discussion about the

---

Even our own government's recent introduction of the Children Act (1989) reflects an intention to take seriously the need both to protect and provide for children. The Act also recognises that there are circumstances when children should have a voice in discussions and decisions about matters which affect their future. It's a reflection of our growing conviction that children are no longer to be 'seen but not heard'. As a society we now recognise that children are people in their own right, with their own particular gifts and needs.

One of the results of the 'emancipation' of children in our society (rightly or wrongly), is that they are more aware of their rights and increasingly unafraid to challenge the ways in which we exclude them.

This emphasis on the rights of children goes hand-in-hand with our growing awareness of the 'moral vacuum' in which many of our children are struggling towards adulthood. One only has to think of recent headline stories (the conviction for murder of two ten-year-old boys; teenage joyriding; reports of extensive school bullying) to be aware that both family life and traditional family values are breaking down.

significance of Confirmation and its traditional role as the entry point into full participation in the life of the church.

Francis Bridger (author of *Children Finding Faith*) is one of many people who, in recent years, have helped us find out more about how children learn about God during their different stages of growth and development. For example, it is now recognised that one of the most significant ways that young children learn is through experience. By copying, mimicking, doing something alongside an adult or older sibling, the child gradually explores, experiences and understands his world. Most teachers are familiar with a perceptive observation from ancient China: 'I hear and I forget; I see and I remember; I do and I understand.'

If experience plays such a vital role in learning and development, are we wise to postpone entry to Communion to the onset of adolescence? Does it make sense to leave something so important to such a late stage in the child's growth?

The evidence of Scripture and the tradition of the church supports the principle of admitting only baptised persons to Communion. However, a passing observation of mine is that in a number of churches (particularly 'gathered' church congregations in city or urban areas) parents have an increasing tendency to opt for a thanksgiving rather than a baptism service. At the same time, there is a growing concern among parents about the place of the child in the whole life of the church. I believe there is an urgent need for the church to give priority to teaching about the importance and meaning of baptism.

Our response

How should the church respond? We can either retreat into our spiritual fortress, or face the tough task of working out new ways of making our faith relevant to today's troubled men, women and children. In the Autumn of 1993, a government minister issued a stinging challenge to the Church of England – what is it doing to teach children the difference between right and wrong? Through my own experience of meeting hundreds of people who are working with families and young children in their churches, I am aware that they are re-evaluating the relevance of their individual ministries to children. But they are also questioning the relevance of the church's large-scale ministry to children. Among the issues they are addressing are all-age worship, more active participation of adults and children in the liturgy and, of course, children and Communion. It is in this context that we need to discuss the admission of children to Communion.

Different Christian traditions place different values and emphases on Communion. Understanding these approaches is a vital link in the process of working out whether or not we should admit our children to Communion before the traditional entry point of Confirmation.

- Traditional Orthodox Christians believe that baptism and Communion should be given at the same time to all who are being initiated, regardless of whether they are children or adults.
- Some churches (many Baptists, for example) delay both the initiation of 'believer's baptism' and the admittance to Communion until adulthood.
- Other churches see baptism as linked to the taking of Communion, in the sense that one prepares for the other. For example, in some traditions children are admitted when they are able to distinguish between the eucharistic bread and ordinary bread. In other traditions children are admitted when they can recognise and be aware of their own sin and are able, in some way, to confess that sin. In these traditions there is a strong emphasis on a period of careful teaching and practical preparation leading to the child's first Communion.

What the Bible does and does not say

Unfortunately the New Testament gives no cut-and-dried

guidance about the participation of children in the Lord's Supper. It does offer, however, two very clear and relevant pictures. The first is of a Saviour who includes and welcomes children. The second is of an early church pattern of all-age participation in the home where 'They devoted themselves to the apostles' teaching and to the fellowship, to the breaking of bread and to prayer. Everyone was filled with awe, and many wonders and miraculous signs were done by the apostles. All the believers were together and had everything in common' (Acts 2:42-44).

Paul's strictures about 'eating or drinking the cup of the Lord in an unworthy manner' (1 Corinthians 11:27-34) are often referred to by those who question the welcoming of baptised children to Communion before Confirmation. However, as with many texts used to support particular arguments, it is important to take the 'there and then' context of this letter into account.

When Paul writes, 'Because there is one loaf, we, who are many, are one body, for we all partake of the one loaf (1 Corinthians 10:17), he is giving a picture of the church being one body sharing in Communion. But in chapter 11 he goes on to show how in the church at Corinth this 'whole body' participation had been violated by the self-centredness of the rich, who indulged themselves in the meal with no concern for the poor. (Communion in the early church was part of a meal that was shared by all – slave and free, adult and child.) The behaviour of this particular group in Corinth aroused Paul's criticism for their lack of a 'servant heart'. They served themselves first, ate greedily and let others go hungry.

Paul's warning concerns the insensitivity of certain members of the body towards others: 'Therefore, whoever eats the bread or drinks the cup of the Lord in an unworthy manner will be guilty of sinning against the body and blood of the Lord... For anyone who eats and drinks without recognising the body of the Lord eats and drinks judgement on himself' (1 Corinthians 11:27, 29).

This passage isn't, I believe, about the admission of children to Communion, but rather about the discipleship of God's people and how they live their lives in a way that honours and serves God and one another. Contemporary commentator Geiko Muller Fahrenholz writes:

> This passage in fact deals with the commitment and discipline of the Eucharistic community. Whenever the community is insensitive to the requirement of transcending human barriers, particularly by favouring the rich, by excluding racial groups, disadvantaged or disabled persons, children or elderly people in its way of life, then that community contradicts the will of God and violates the eucharist because it does not discern the body.

What about preparation for Communion?

Many who oppose admitting children to Communion fear that adequate teaching about the meaning of Communion will disappear. Those in favour argue that what matters is instructing children in their faith in a way that is appropriate to their age and stage of development – emotional, mental, physical as well as spiritual.

Opponents of the admission of young children also fear the undermining of the child's voluntary decision. Who will decide the appropriate 'starting age'? Will it be constant throughout the church, or will it vary from congregation to congregation?

I believe that such fear is rooted in the belief that adults and children will assume that admission to the Communion table is a matter of right, rather than of a voluntary offering of themselves to God.

Along with all who are in favour of admitting children to Communion, I believe that they are progressing on a journey of faith and that they must be supported, encouraged and helped to make their own voluntary decision when the time is right for them. I believe our adult responsibility is to keep the doors of opportunity open and to nurture and instruct children in the ways of faith.

Opponents argue that young children will not understand

Long Term Experiment

It is now almost ten years since the establishment in a number of dioceses of 'experimental parishes', where children have been able to take Communion before Confirmation. I find it significant that even after ten years, these are still deemed 'experiments'!

In a recent survey of ninety-eight of these parishes, almost eighty per cent of them were convinced of the positive value of admitting children to Communion before Confirmation (*Communion Before Confirmation*, a report on the survey conducted by Culham College Institute, 1993, Culham Educational Foundation, p.34).

The wide variety of practice across the churches and even within particular denominations, is extremely bewildering – for children and for adults! I have to admit that I rather warm to the Methodists' 1987 guidelines, *Children at Holy Communion*, in which the Methodist Church Division of Education and Youth 'invites local churches to use the guidelines actively to encourage the fuller participation of children in the Lord's Supper'. Many of us who are theologically committed to including children would welcome similar practical guidelines.

repentance and therefore will not be able to make their confession before partaking in Communion. Those in favour argue that young children can come to Communion with a real sense of theirs and others' wrongdoing, and that they can both say and mean that they are sorry. Of course, with very young children repentance will be felt, rather than verbalised with complete intellectual self-awareness.

The fundamental question is whether young children should be excluded from Communion simply because they cannot put into words what they actually feel, experience and know.

Where are you now?

Here are some statements about children's experience of Communion. How do they reflect current practice in your church?

- They are barely aware of Communion because they stay outside in their children's groups or are only in church for a small part of the service.
- They sit with their children's groups while the adults receive Communion.
- They sit with their parents and go with them or sit with them as the adults receive Communion.
- They come to the rail and they are blessed/prayed with/ prayed for.
- They are welcomed to Communion, where the parents share the bread with them.
- The children are given their own bread and wine.

It is clear that there is a wide spectrum of practice, ranging from total exclusion, through semi-involvement, to full welcome. I believe that because we have a pastoral responsibility for our children, we owe it to them to pursue a more consistent and coherent policy with regard to their participation in Communion.

Where do you want to get to?

What are the implications for the church if children are admitted to Communion?

- It will test the church about how inclusive and welcoming it is.
- Liturgy, both spoken and sung, will need to be more accessible for children. Simple language, use of repetition, identifiable pattern and sequence will be important. Liturgical renewal may also call for a more frequent pattern of Communion Services.

- Adults' superiority will be challenged and it will call us to rediscover the 'servanthood' nature of the church, which calls us to 'honour our weaker members' (1 Corinthians 12:21-26).
- All-age services will need to be accepted as a valued part of church life rather than seen as an optional extra for families only.
- Congregations will need to take a more defined, corporate responsibility for the children – they will need to be 'corporate godparents'!
- The church will need to produce creative parish resources (including videos, workbooks, sound and visual aids) that will help prepare young children to participate in the Communion Service.
- At a local level, diocesan and other church organisations will need to train service leaders and lay preachers in the leading of all-age services.
- At a national level, theological colleges should provide a variety of courses, including:
Teaching and leading worship in an all-age context.
The spiritual development of the child.
The child and Communion: theological and practical issues, including preparing a child for Communion.

In conclusion

Beliefs affect actions. Asking whether we should admit children to Communion is much more than a question of liturgical procedure. It forces us to examine two difficult and controversial issues: the value and status of children before God and the nature and significance of the Communion Service. It's hardly surprising that church leaders have preferred to postpone making a decision.

Meshed in with the theological issues is our ongoing pastoral responsibility for the nurture of our children as they make their respective journeys of faith.

It is vitally important that we respond to what we know about children – for example, we know that they learn through experience. Then we may argue that children discover their place in the body, following baptism, by being treated as valued, participating members. Others may argue that their membership only truly begins when they are old enough to articulate and profess their faith.

I'm encouraged that the church appears to be changing its position about children – for example, the Church of Scotland has recently agreed to admit children to Communion. Or maybe the church is simply becoming a little more open about admitting its confusion! It is good that children are much more welcome in Communion Services than they have been.

If we take children seriously, then we have a responsibility to explore seriously how welcome children really are in the church. That exploration will lead us to ask hard questions about how we welcome children when we gather to commemorate the death and resurrection of Christ in the service of Holy Communion.

What more awe-inspiring experience could there be for a child than to be with other members of the body as they remember what Christ has done for them, respond in confession, receive forgiveness and give their thanks?

I can't help but remember that Jesus welcomed little children with open arms – will we?

CHAPTER SIX

SERVING CHILDREN THROUGH RELATIONSHIPS

The relationship factor

'No man is an island,' said John Donne, Dean of St Paul's, in a famous poem. He was right! I'd simply add, neither is any woman, boy or girl! Being a Christian is about being connected to our fellow-believers. We live, learn and grow in a wonderfully intricate network made of people. We are one body, sharing the same life. Each part has tremendous integrity. None has complete independence. You can sum it up in one word – relationship.

I believe our main purpose as Christians is to worship God with the whole of our lives. We are called to do this both individually and corporately. If the adults in the congregation are not convinced of this and are reluctant to make worship a priority, then it will hardly be surprising if the children find it difficult as well.

We may sing songs and say prayers enthusiastically, but we will not be led into worship that opens us up to God and one another. A key factor in enabling this to happen is the quality of existing relationships in the local church. When we introduce even the youngest children into church, we are welcoming them into God's family, which has a particular calling to relate to one another as brothers and sisters, regardless of age or status.

Jesus explained to his followers that all those who do the will of the Father are members of a new family: 'Whoever does God's will is my brother and sister and mother' (Mark 3:35). And Hebrews 13:1 tells us: 'Keep on loving each other as brothers.'

To belong to Jesus means that I belong to a new body, the church. I not only have a dependent relationship with Jesus, but also an *interdependent* relationship with all those who are members of his body: 'From him the whole body, joined and held together by every supporting ligament, grows and builds itself up in love, as each part does its work' (Ephesians 4:16).

Being members of a new family gives us new privileges and responsibilities and a whole new way of relating to one another. If children are to be welcomed into the church as fellow-pilgrims, we also need to welcome them into our relationships. This has all sorts of implications.

Creating meaningful relationships with children

I want to challenge adults not only to agree that they should take children seriously, but also to show that agreement practically through a commitment to befriending, helping and actively supporting their younger brothers and sisters. First of all we need to believe that such relationships are a possibility – and then do everything we can to realise them.

- We need to pray for this to happen.
- We need to look for opportunities and ways to develop healthy and helpful relationships between adult members of the congregation and children and young people.
- We need to identify the barriers which prevent communication between the different age groups.
- We need to plan and offer programmes of events where all ages can work, play or mix together.
- We need to take an honest look how the different generations relate to each other (or fail to relate to each other) in our churches. Have we developed a form of 'age segregation' in

our activities and worship? What natural opportunities exist for different ages to mix together?

Healthy relationships among church members can make all the difference to children, whatever background they come from. They act as a beacon to them, demonstrating a way of life that is based on radically different priorities and values from the world in which they are growing up.

Sometimes we forget how very different Christian values are from those of late twentieth-century secular society. Christ's church turns society upside-down, reversing conventional notions of status. It takes menial servanthood as its model of leadership. Because its sole basis of membership is free undeserved grace, the church, if it is true to itself, is going to be a place where today's 'achievement oriented' thinking is challenged.

In *Public Values and Corporate Life*, a paper my husband wrote in 1990, he states: 'It is my belief that our congregation has been deeply influenced by free-market ideology...' This 'me first' way of thinking, he argues, directly undermines our corporate life. Many of the values promoted by government in particular and society in general are ones that subtly undermine both our corporate life and the quality of our relationships with one another.

In our life together we are called to live in interdependence, and with integrity. If we are to act as a genuine 'visual aid' of the kingdom, then I believe that we need:

- To be aware of the undermining nature of the society around us.
- To pray for the re-establishing of healthy corporate relationships in the church.
- To guard against 'pulling up the drawbridge' and defensively retreating from the world and all its evil ways.
- To look for ways of demonstrating the difference which Christian values make by engaging with the world around us.

In this we will be backed by the strength and protection of our corporate relationships in Christ.

An 'alternative' way of living

In his book *Call to Conversion*, Jim Wallis writes: 'We have nothing more to share with the world than we are sharing with each other. We can effect no change in the ways of the world unless we ourselves are being converted from those ways.'

I believe that implicit in that challenge is a call to review the quality of relationships in the church between adults and children. And while it's important that we face up to issues of, say, women's ministry and Communion for children, I believe it's equally vital that we address the following 'background' questions too:

- How much have we 'bought into' the pervading values of our culture?
- How much of our corporate life has been undermined, particularly in relationship to the significance which God gives to children?
- How can we be restored to the community to which God calls us?

I am not interested in encouraging people merely to tolerate children. I want something far more positive. I want my fellow-Christians to recognise that we *need* our younger brothers and sisters in the body in order to experience growth and development in our own Christian lives. If we avoid contact with them, or responsibility for them, then we rob ourselves of potential spiritual growth – something that God intends us to have as we learn to value, accept, encourage and affirm our younger brothers and sisters in the body. In order to face this challenge we need to be convinced that:

- God intends us to be in relationship with our younger brothers and sisters in the church.

● God intends us to serve the children, whatever that may mean in practice in our particular situations.

Serving the children

What does that mean in practice? The possibilities are endless – anything from involvement in running holiday clubs, week-by-week children's work, praying for a particular school situation or organising a football club.

Some of the boys in our children's work at York wanted more physical activity than was practicable during their Sunday morning group. So, as a way of serving these lads, the adults in our church organised and trained a football team for eight- to eleven-year-olds. I remain indebted to the group of men who not only committed themselves to give their time, but also their pastoral and spiritual support as the needs arose. As I write, I can see the certificate the team presented to me when I left. It is signed by the leaders and it reads:

St Michael's Workshop Football Club

This is to certify that
Jackie Cray
was appointed
Honorary Life President

I have to admit that it is a very precious and prized possession!

Priority of resources

Children are indispensable to the life of the church. Recognition of this fact may involve some hard thinking about where they come in our scale of priorities. How do we resource their needs? Maybe, to redress a long-standing imbalance, we need to introduce an element of 'positive discrimination' in their favour.

What happens in your church when, say, a new gifted guitarist

Food For Thought

One Sunday we looked at the theme of 'Serving one another in the church.' We explored what it means in basic, practical terms to serve one another in the body of Christ. We felt it important to take into account our individual situation with its various mission and caring involvements. We looked at all our activities. We noted where the children were already involved in serving the life of the church. For example, several children, including our two daughters, helped serve breakfasts and lunches with a team of adults working with homeless people. We also thought about new possibilities of involvement for them.

We decided on some messy foot-painting to communicate our ideas of what being part of the body meant. We drew some large outlines of the church building on a huge sheet of paper. Then the children took off their socks, dipped their feet in some paint and 'put themselves in the picture'! Or at least they put their footprints into the drawing of the church building. This is definitely not an exercise for the faint-hearted. It needs careful pre-planning, lots of bowls of clean water, towels and extra pairs of hands to help mop up!

As we had messy feet and bowls of water, we found we had the ideal opportunity to serve one another by washing one another's feet. After some initial giggling and embarrassment, the children set about the task, which ended by having a profound effect on us all. Looking back, I see it as a 'landmark' event, symbolising our commitment to a more open and inclusive attitude to our younger brothers and sisters.

What about some foot-washing with the whole congregation? Could you use it as an activity on a church 'fun' day or even as part of the family service?

arrives? Does she get channelled into the work with the sevens to elevens group? Or is she more likely to be assigned to the 'top' end of the youth work, or invited to play in the main worship services?

How many churches give priority of leadership resources to their work with children? If we don't channel 'quality' Christian teachers, worship leaders, organisers and pastors into the children's work and worship, then I believe we will be missing much of what God purposes for them.

I believe that children should be treated with higher honour and therefore need to be given higher priority in our churches' schemes and plans. That involves everything from including them in the mission statement, drawing up a proper budget for the children's work, to the implementation of a policy for directing more leaders into that work. As well as pressing for a priority of resources for the children, we also need to explore how much children actually feel they belong in the whole life of the church.

The benefits of belonging

How can children belong to the body? Their most basic qualification for membership is the fact that Christ died for them. Also, as a committed Anglican, I believe that baptism affirms their belonging to God's family in a public act of welcome. Too often, we pay this little more than lip service. In practical day-to-day terms, of course, children belong where they are made to feel they belong.

One of the high points of the Cray family's summer is our annual trip to Greenbelt, the open-air Christian arts festival. For years now my two daughters' greatest ambition has been to have a back-stage pass. Much as they enjoy being in the audience 'out front', a pass would get them into the heart of the action, where they could experience the hustle and bustle of setting up the stage for the various artists. They'd also have the thrill of face-to-face meetings with their favourite performers. So, imagine their frustration if, having been given a back-stage pass, they were told they were not allowed to use it.

A crazy state of affairs! But isn't that rather like the way we treat our children? They may have baptism certificates, membership badges for their group activities, or any other token of being recognised as part of the church. But they will not experience the benefits of belonging unless their adult brothers and sisters in the church relate to them, welcome them and accept them on a regular basis.

There are a number of ways we can encourage this sense of belonging. One of them is to look at how we create and sustain relationships in the shared life of the church.

Creating and sustaining relationships

● We need to believe God intends us to do this.

● We need to believe that God equips us to do this by his Spirit.

● We need to be committed to the members of our church and make a regular effort to get to know them.

● We need to be prayerful, asking for God's leading and wisdom about how and where to put that commitment.

In what ways – practical as well as spiritual – can we encourage different parts of the body to act as part of the whole? Take a look at 1 Corinthians 12:1-27 and discuss it as a family, a house group, play leaders, youth and children's workers or a church staff team. Ask yourself:

● How do we experience being part of the body of Christ in our church?
● Are children in our church considered to be part of the body?
● How are children related to in the life of the church?

In answering these questions, you will begin to measure how welcoming and inclusive you are towards children. But this begs questions. How can we begin to build a network of healthy relationships to incorporate the children? Where and how do we build our relationships with the children in the church?

111

The command of Christ is: 'Love one another. As I have loved you, so you must love one another' (John 13:34). How do we begin to fulfil this with the children in the church?

In St John's first letter we read that we ought to lay down our lives for our brethren. This involves, among other things, meeting their material needs – loving in action and in truth, loving in obedience to God and in response to his Spirit at work in us.

First, we need to be open to God's Spirit and his prompting. Secondly, we need to be open to God concerning how he wants us to serve the children in the church, both practically and spiritually. Thirdly, we need to have courage to get on with the job while actively seeking the support and involvement of other members of the church.

In many ways our present lifestyle makes it easier for us to build relationships, at least at certain levels. Today's young people are more sure of themselves. Women are learning to be more assertive, expecting to be heard and listened to in relationships. Men are encouraged to share their feelings as well as their intellect. We are a mobile society and therefore we have had to develop skills for initiating relationships more quickly.

At the same time, however, our society is increasingly achievement-oriented and self-pleasing. It seems to be getting harder for adults and children to think and act in a way that considers others. Those of us who are teachers notice this in the classroom with children of all ages, in their work and at play. A very experienced head of a nursery school commented to me that she was more and more aware of the lack of social skills in children entering her nursery. She observed that the only means the children seemed to have for resolving conflicts, large and small, was to act in a violent and aggressive manner both physically and verbally to children and teachers alike.

Talk and listen

In family situations, take time to talk about issues and listen to

112

one another. Our children are sometimes so vocal that they don't allow others to have their say. Be willing to set some limits, particularly when getting together in small groups. Try giving the speaker a small ball or an orange – or any small object – which he or she may hold for an agreed time, say five minutes, during which time no one may interrupt. In this way each person may have a platform.

Be clear about your boundaries. We often have to keep our nerve as parents and be willing to be firm about certain limits while being flexible about others. A friend recently said that in her experience of bringing up three teenagers of very different personalities and needs, the boundaries could change weekly. Be aware of one another's differences, whether it's of temperament or upbringing, and be willing to honour, love and serve one another in places of difference and conflict as well as of agreement.

We tend to build relationships where we feel comfortable, where we are welcomed and where we find we have certain things in common. The gospel challenges us to love one another despite differences. This means that God's people need to make a conscious commitment to love one another in the church. This takes us beyond greeting one another in the peace, to becoming involved prayerfully and practically in one another's lives. It makes us aware of one another's differences as we learn to respect and honour one another in spite of them. Christian love is not sentimental. I know that as an adult I find loving my fellow-Christians far from easy. I know children do as well.

Relationship-building is particularly hard when we don't understand or know where someone is 'coming from'. But when we take time to listen to that person and find out some of his personal and spiritual journey, then we begin to understand and maybe appreciate him.

My question is, 'Where in our church lives do we make space to do that with the children?' It may happen in the children's work and it may happen to some extent between families, but where do the adult members of the church, single and married, male and female, get an opportunity to mix with, talk with, play with and listen to children?

In society we have stopped segregating the sexes, but we still seem eager to segregate children and adults. It is true that in church we worship together (some of the time), but there seem to be few opportunities for members of the church to meet across the age barriers.

Why, where and how?

● Are the leaders of your church convinced that the Bible teaches us that we should be in good and right relationships with one another in the body of Christ?

● Are the leaders of your church convinced that children are included in those relationships?

● How is this achieved in terms of your church's planning and programme of events?

● What specific events are planned that mix the age groups?

● Have you thought, as a church, about planning an all-age event, to explore a particular theme or teaching – for example, to celebrate Easter, Christmas or Harvest?

● Or, have you thought about looking at a journey of faith (the story of Abraham, for example) and including in it examples from the 'faith journeys' of a whole variety of members of the congregation, regardless of age?

Coffee time

My experience of serving coffee and cold drinks after church is that it is a great opportunity for the adults to meet one another. On the whole the children find it boring, unless they are involved in some way, giving out the drinks, serving biscuits, mounting and displaying work from their groups and classes. They are happier if there is some comfortable place where they can be with each

---

A Few Ideas For All-Age Events

- Harvest supper.
- Missionary evening.
- Picnic, games and treasure hunt in a local park.
- Barbecue.
- An organised walk.
- An outing to the local swimming pool (you can hire them by the hour and also a room to have lunch or tea in afterwards).
- Helping children to organise a *Blue Peter*-style bring and buy event.
- Raising money and support for a special project.

---

other – for example, a corner with some large cushions, small chairs and a selection of books and games. Often by the end of a service, small children are very fed up, suffering from a combination of boredom and tiredness. It would be a shame if adults lost the opportunity to be together because no one had put any thought into making the 'after-church' time pleasant for children.

Having a shared lunch together straight after church is one way of starting to mix the age groups. Nothing elaborate – it could be a 'bring your own' sort of picnic (only in the church hall), or just sandwiches and cakes. For the children's sake it's better if it's shorter rather than longer, unless your church buildings are the sort of place with lots of play equipment and creative resources. How often you do this will depend on your congregational mix – monthly, every six weeks, or maybe more often in the summer. It's a great opportunity to introduce new folk to the church, and it helps children feel more at home, because they begin to recognise people and to be recognised themselves.

Giving and receiving in relationships

Organised events are only one way of fostering relationships. They grow when people engage in discussion, planning or shared problem-solving. They grow when people play together, or have to learn to co-operate together in order to reach a decision. They grow when people learn to receive from one another as well as to give.

All of this applies to children as well. Children grow in relationship, when they are given the opportunity to relate. It's obvious! I remember an occasion when my older daughter wanted to invite a young autistic friend to her birthday party. Conventional speech is not Barry's preferred method of communication, but that didn't make any difference to their friendship. Catherine and Barry understood each other well enough.

Other parents were unsure of how their children would relate to Barry at the party. I think the reason was connected to the fact that they themselves did not know how to communicate and relate. Once Catherine had introduced her friends to Barry, you would have thought that those children had related all their lives!

The sad truth is that we are often similarly unsure, insecure and lacking in confidence in our relationships in the church, especially with people who are 'different'. Fortunately it is also true that children have a special ability to build bridges with those who are different, as long as we give them a secure base from which to start.

Any healthy relationship is a two-way street. It involves giving and receiving. How can we both give and receive in our relationships with our children – particularly in a way that goes beyond the sort of interaction that happens between them and their own group leaders?

● Are there opportunities in our church life for adults to engage in relationship with children outside of the structured children's work?

● Are there the opportunities to learn and receive spiritually from our younger brothers and sisters?

● Do we believe that our younger brothers and sisters have spiritual wisdom and gifts worth sharing with all?

We may give children opportunities to be with other members of the church, even (daring thought!) to have fun with other members of the church – which I happen to believe is very important and healthy for our relationships. We may also be willing to listen to children and be genuinely open to their needs. But a church will not progress in its relationship with children unless the members, God's people, are vulnerable, humble and willing to learn, even from the very young.

Eli was willing to be like this in his relationship with Samuel – open to God working and speaking in unexpected and different ways, including through a young child (see 1 Samuel 3). If we are to learn with and from children, we need to be open to creative and different ways of looking at things. We must be willing to receive the truth from unexpected places. We may be open to a child serving us with tea and biscuits in the church hall – but are we equally open to receiving spiritual gifts from children, in the context of a network of healthy relationships?

Children and spiritual gifts

Spiritual gifts are not just a wacky idea the charismatics came up with, but a central New Testament theme. The following points are taken from *Tools for the Job – An Introductory Teaching Course on Spiritual Gifts*, by the Church Pastoral Aid Society:

● All ministry and mission originates from Christ, including spiritual gifts.

● Christ gives the gifts of the Spirit (Ephesians 4:8).

● The gifts are given to each Christian (1 Corinthians 12:7).

● Spiritual gifts are to be understood within a particular context of corporate relationships. The New Testament portrays this corporate fellowship as safe yet vulnerable, secure yet open and accountable.

● Spiritual gifts are given to be shared among the body of Christ.

● There are varieties of gifts (1 Corinthians 12:4-11, 27-30; Romans 12:6-8; 1 Peter 4:10).

● Gifts have both a natural and supernatural element.

● No Christian is meant to have all the gifts. As a body of believers, we are meant to complement one another's gifts and ministries.

● Gifts require human co-operation. One evangelist said he was born with the 'gift of the gab' and God turned it into a gift of evangelism.

● Not all spiritual gifts are a special anointing of our natural abilities. All gifts require our human co-operation, but some, like healing, are more directly God's activity through us.

● As gifts are recognised and understood, patterns of gifting will emerge.

Most importantly, are you open to whatever gift the Holy Spirit wants to give you? You cannot easily lead children into something that is not within your experience.

Let me describe something which happened in our children's work a few years ago and had particular relevance to the life of the wider church.

It was Palm Sunday 1990. Our five- to ten-year-olds had been learning about the events leading up to Good Friday. During our worship time, one of our children (a ten-year-old) had a 'mind's eye' picture of a blood orange with a band around it – rather like a Christingle orange – but the band around this orange was white, unlike the red band of the Christingle. There was red juice coming out of the top of the blood orange, trickling down the side and seeping into the white band around the orange. Instead of the white band being stained red by the juice, the band grew whiter and whiter as the juice soaked into it.

Leaders and children listened and reflected on this. We felt that through this picture God was showing us what had been accomplished at Calvary. There was a real sense of awe at what Jesus had done in shedding his blood for us, so that our sins would no longer be scarlet but whiter than snow!

The picture was a better 'visual aid' than anything the children's leaders could have thought up, and it had a far greater spiritual impact on the children as a whole. The children took this sense of awe and wonder into the following family service, where they were able to respond in praise and thankfulness for Jesus and his coming into Jerusalem on that first Palm Sunday.

The children's leaders all felt this picture was significant. They shared it with the leaders of the service, who in turn shared it with the whole church. From responses after the service we knew that many people were both challenged and helped by this picture that had come from a young child.

It would have been so easy to brush that child's contribution to one side. We might easily have missed what God wanted to share with us as a whole church. I am glad that the children were given the opportunity to receive from God, and that they were able to share his simple message with the whole church.

Tools for the job

My husband Graham has written:

> The gifts of the Spirit are the tools God gives to his people for their part in establishing his kingdom. They are God's ways of building up the church and continuing the ministry of Jesus to the world. They are the tangible ways in which we minister our life in Christ to one another and to the society in which we live. Without them there is no ministry and no mission.

Are we to understand that these tools are for God's adult people only? Or are they for the children as well? At Pentecost, Peter tells the people that what they are witnessing is not a crowd of drunken men, but rather the fulfilment of what the prophet Joel foretold about the pouring out of the Spirit: 'In the last days, God says, I will pour out my Spirit on all people. Your sons and daughters will prophesy, your young men will see visions, your old men will dream dreams' (Acts 2:17).

I believe that the Holy Spirit, who is sent to reveal Jesus to us and to minister the power and gifts of God through us, *is* available to our children (brought up and nurtured in the faith) as well as to adults. Therefore children as well as adults may minister the life of Christ to one another. This must, of course, be within the same restraints as any adult ministry of the gifts of the Spirit.

Here are some guidelines for the giving and receiving of spiritual gifts:

● The gifts are given/administered in a way that is honouring to the person or the body of believers.
● Those regularly administering spiritual gifts need to place themselves under the spiritual and pastoral authority of the leaders of the church.
● Those ministering spiritual gifts need to be living their personal and public lives according to God's Word.
● Those administering gifts need to be open to correction.
● The bringer of the gift needs to be rooted in the life of the church.
● Spiritual gifts must be consistent with Scripture.
● The manner in which spiritual gifts are ministered is important; they need to be ministered in love.
● The leaders and the body of believers have a responsibility to test and weigh the gifts.
● In the actual ministering of the gift Jesus is seen to be exalted, rather than the giver of the gift.

There should also be an assessment of the 'result' of any gift. The following questions may be useful aids to assessment when someone brings a word or message which he or she believes is from God.

- Did members of the congregation know or have an inner conviction that they were hearing the voice of the Spirit?
- Did the message build up the church or just give someone a 'voice'?
- If it was a prediction, was it fulfilled?

These tests should be applied to children who are ministering spiritual gifts on a regular and recognised basis. There should also be simple and accessible teaching about the weighing and testing of gifts. And, of course, there should be careful and sensitive pastoral supervision.

We had a number of children in York who were particularly gifted. We were careful to guard and nurture these children, teaching and explaining from Scripture as they experienced the gifts of the Spirit, sometimes in unexpected pictures, 'words' and experiences. We never felt it right to expose any of the children in church and put them 'up front'. If we sensed a word or picture was something for the whole church, one of the leaders of the service would share it, saying which age group it had come from. We never gave the child's name. I think we need to be very careful to avoid over-exposing the spiritually gifted among us, particularly the children.

Recommended reading

Call to Conversion, Jim Wallis, Harper & Row: San Francisco, 1992

Tools for the Job – An Introductory Teaching Course on Spiritual Gifts, the Church Pastoral Aid Society, 1990

Young Saints – living in the power of the Spirit, a teaching course for eight- to eleven-year-olds, Alan Price, Anglican Renewal Ministries, 1993

And For Your Children, Chris and John Leach, Monarch Publications, 1994

CHAPTER SEVEN

A NEW WAY OF LOOKING

Puzzling pictures

Crazes come and go. Do you remember struggling in frustration with Rubik's Cube? Recently I've noticed a wave of popularity for a new, and equally absorbing pastime – looking at the 'magic eye' pictures, which, in book form and as posters, are currently selling in their thousands.

At first glance there is no picture at all. All you see is a mass of loosely patterned coloured squiggles. But, as my daughter assured me, the 'surface' image hides an intriguing and astonishingly vivid three-dimensional picture. The trick is in learning how to look at it.

My daughter encouraged me to relax and not focus my eyes on the nearest point, but to imagine I was looking *through* the surface patterns, as I might through a window, and focus there instead. Probably rather too eagerly I tried to look through and beyond the squiggles and – guess what I saw? – more patterned, coloured squiggles! While everyone else was gasping in amazement at what they could see, I was left wondering what all the fuss was about. What was it I should be seeing, and why was it that I couldn't see it?

But I persisted and at last, as I placed my nose against the surface of the picture, it suddenly happened. The surface disappeared and I was looking into a deep, brightly coloured space – and there, floating in it, were three large, three-dimensional green tropical fish. In its small way, it was a revelation, a breath-taking moment, revealing something that so easily could have remained hidden to me. Now, of course, I'm one of the initiates, and it takes me only a moment to 'focus in' on a new picture to discover the secret that lies beneath the surface. All I needed was *to learn how to look* at the picture in a new way.

Learning to look

God is in the business of changing the way we look at things. The Christian life is a day-by-day, lifelong process of allowing him, through the power of his Holy Spirit, to change our fallen human perspective. The 'kingdom values' which Jesus proclaimed are the 'corrective lenses' which will help us see the world from his point of view – a radical prescription which turns conventional human perception upside-down.

God is forever giving us new ways of looking at things. At the personal level, it may be the growing realisation and acknowledgement that the way I behave (and *am*) in a relationship contributes to the health, stability and growth of that relationship. Sometimes it's that painful, humbling moment when we see ourselves 'as others see us'. Or it may be that moment which sometimes comes after long, prayer-filled struggles with a particular problem – the realisation that what needs to change is not so much the problem itself, but my attitude towards it.

At other times God may challenge us about the way we view the 'big picture', demanding that we step back and become aware of some of the underlying social, political and economic forces which shape our lives. Recently I've been profoundly challenged about my attitudes to poverty, both at home and overseas, and about my willingness to commit myself to supporting action for change.

The 'vision thing'

Family. This book has been all about ways of looking. I've argued for a fresh, biblically-based re-examination of what it means to be a family. I've suggested that we should widen our definition to reflect the open, inclusive family values of both Old and New Testaments. We need to be willing to remove some of the barriers that have for too long prevented us from learning what it means to be vulnerable to one another.

The church. Our definition of family will shape our definition of the church. Think small and it will continue to be the place where I go 'to have my needs met', a kind of spiritual garage where each individual drops in for a weekly refill and oil-change, for minor repairs and a tune-up. Step back and the picture changes, becoming multi-dimensional. Individuals are still clearly visible, but suddenly we start to see how we are meant to relate to each other in the body of Christ. We will continue, of course, to have our needs met – but in a context of interdependence, not independence. It's an exciting prospect – and an unnerving one as well. It goes completely against the grain of everything that the twentieth century has taught us about the supremacy of the individual.

Children. For too long the conventional picture has been of 'us' and 'them'. 'Us', the adults, are firmly in the foreground and 'them', the children and young people, are in their traditional place – at the back, or hidden somewhere in the larger picture of church life. In terms of priorities, resources, teaching and pastoral care, the focus on the adults is fairly clear, but somewhat more fuzzy on the children.

But step back and, as with the 'magic eye' images, the picture changes completely. The adults are still there and so are the children, but suddenly the focus is more evenly distributed. The different age groups are mixing together, serving one another, learning from one another. Because they are acknowledged as fellow-pilgrims sharing the same journey of faith with their adult

124

brothers and sisters, the children's place within the community is assured. They are recognised, valued and included. Their needs neither come first nor last on the agenda, but are there simply as a matter of right, rather than sufferance.

Community. As we catch a new vision of the wonderful inclusiveness of the body of Christ, other more compartmentalised ways of seeing and thinking will begin to fade. Traditional labels (single/married, young/old, disabled, unemployed etc) will become less important and we will honour and receive one another as those who share an equal status in Christ – that of beloved children, whatever our age. In this new vision I see a renewed church, empowered by the Spirit, and shaped by the word of God, a welcoming church to young and old, small and big, rich and poor, a church actively encouraging children of all ages to be both seen and heard, in his eternal presence. In this way we shall become a little more like the extraordinary, world-changing, world-challenging community that Jesus charged us to be.

Into action

There's nothing more exciting than a revelatory moment of vision. Putting that vision into practice is another matter altogether. One holiday Sunday, a number of years ago, our church in York was packed with visitors. Many of them had come hoping to hear our well-known minister David Watson speak. As it turned out the preacher was one of our lay readers. With his customary dry Scottish wit, he began his sermon by saying, 'Well, I guess many of you came here today hoping to hear David Watson, but instead you've got me. You came for strawberries and cream and you end up getting plums and custard! And it will do you just as much good.'

The nitty-gritty work of transforming vision into practice may sometimes feel more like plums and custard than strawberries and cream. Certainly it's less glamorous – but 'where there is no vision, the people perish' (Proverbs 29:18). The Bible tells us that vision and 'working out' are twin activities – if you like, strawberries and cream and plums and custard both belong on our menu. Both will sustain us as we seek to welcome and include children in the church.

In this book I've offered a view of how things might be in the life of the church if we 'grasp' a vision for acknowledging children's right to be among us as valued participants. As well as sketching in the biblical background, I hope that I have provided you with some thoughts and practical ideas that may help shape this vision in your church and see it become a reality.

I hope that aspects of this book will be as challenging for you as they have been for me in writing them. I hope that for some of you, the way you think about children in the life of the church will be changed. I hope that others will want to become involved in making the practical changes needed in order for our churches to become places where our children can actively be encouraged to take their place in the whole of the congregation.

In this book I have offered a view of how things might be in the life of the church if we 'grasp' a vision for acknowledging children's rights to be among us as valued participants. I began with the 'imaginary' congregation of St William's: a church which welcomes children and takes them seriously, a church which considers the nurture of all ages as vital, a church which seeks to be imaginative and flexible in its liturgy as well as its teaching, and a church which actively builds relationships across the generations.

I hope that you are convinced biblically and theologically that children are people to be valued and welcomed into the whole life of the church, not just into our church services. I hope that I have provided you with some thoughts and practical ideas that help to shape this vision in *your* church.

I have found this book challenging to write because at each step I have needed to examine not just my theory, reflection and observation, but – for the integrity of the gospel – my practice of it. I hope that you will be similarly challenged about your view of children and any gap that may exist in your personal life as well as in your church life between belief and practice. I hope that for some of you, indeed many of you, the way you think about children in the life of the church will be enlarged, maybe even changed. I hope that others of you will become involved in the practical changes needed in order for our churches to become places where our children can actively be encouraged to take their place in the life of the whole congregation.

We can all start somewhere. Will you take up the challenge to pray, plan and prepare for children to take their rightful place in the church where they will be welcomed and nurtured? Will you dare to believe with me that this is not just an 'impossible dream' but a valid ministry that God calls us to and which he equips us for, through the work of his grace and in the power of the Spirit?